CW01034135

POLISH WINGS

Lechosław Musiałkowski

Petlyakov

Pe-2 & UPe-2

Tupolev USB

STRATUS

Polish Wings

Wydawnictwo STRATUS s.j.
Po. Box 123, 27-600 Sandomierz 1, Poland
phone. 0-15 833 30 41
e-mail: office@stratusbooks.pl
www.stratusbooks.com.pl www.mmpbooks.biz

Copyright © 2019 Stratus,
Copyright © 2019 Lechosław Musiałkowski

ISBN 978-83-65958-42-6

Layout concept	Bartłomiej Belcarz
Cover concept	Artur Juszczak
Cover	Marcin Górecki
Translation	Jarosław Dobrzyński
Proofreading	Roger Wallsgrove
DTP	Bartłomiej Belcarz
Colour Drawings	Karolina Hołda
Edited by	Roger Wallsgrove

PRINTED IN POLAND

All rights reserved. Apart from any fair dealing for the purpose of private study, research, criticism or review, as permitted under the Copyright, Design and Patents Act, 1988, no part of this publication may be reproduced, stored in a retrieval system, or transmitted in any form or by any means, electronic, electrical, chemical, mechanical, optical, photocopying, recording or otherwise, without prior written permission. All enquiries should be addressed to the publisher.

The authors would like to thank the following persons and institutions for their assistance in their work on the book, and for providing photographs and documents.

Photographs from the archive of Marian Mikołajczuk (taken in the Military Photographic Agency and Aviation Institute) and from collections of Tadeusz Bacdorf, Czesław Gagajek, Andrzej Glass, Kazimierz Gawron, Wacław Hołyś, Mariusz Konarski, Ryszard Mierzwiński, Grzegorz Skomorowski, Kazimierz Wierzbicki and Jan Wilkosz, and from archives of Bartłomiej Belcarz, Robert Gretzyngier including photographs taken by Stanisław Borowiecki/PAP, Zygmunt Gruszczyk, Eligiusz Hirnle, Kazimierz Jamrozik, Krzysztof Kirschenstein, Mariusz Konarski, Tadeusz Królikiewicz, Stanisław Maciejewski, Roman Marcinkiewicz, Aleksander Milart, Andrzej Morgała, Wojciech Sankowski, Barbara and Wojciech Sopyłło, Adam Wierzykowski, Józef Zieliński and Konrad Zienkiewicz.

Special thanks to Bartłomiej Belcarz, Kazimierz Gawron, Robert Gretzyngier, Wacłw Hołyś, Krzysztof Kirschenstein, Mariusz Konarski, Andrzej Morgała, Wojciech Sankowski, Krzysztof Sikora and Józef Zieliński for their help at various stages of work.

AVAILABLE

FORTHCOMING

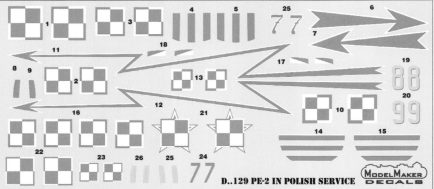

D..129 PE-2 IN POLISH SERVICE

FPHU Model Maker
ul. Lotnicza 13/2, 78-100 Kołobrzeg, Poland
phone. +48 507-024-077
www.modelmaker.com.pl

Petlyakov Pe-2

The history of the development of the Pe-2 started in 1938. It was then that, in the prison Central Design Bureau (TsKB-29) supervised by NKVD, design work was commenced on the prototype of twin engine high altitude fighter aircraft VI-100 (*Vysotnyi Istrebitel*, called also Aircraft 100, *sotka* – after *Spetsalnyi Tekhnicheskiy Otdyel*, Special Technical Department). The design team was supervised by Vladimir M. Petlyakov. The designed aircraft, of all-metal construction with a crew of two, was intended for operations at high altitude, therefore it was to feature a pressurized cockpit, heavy armament and large fuel capacity for long endurance. The VI-100, powered by two Klimov M-105R engines and two TK-3 turbochargers then under development, was to attain a speed of 630 km/h at 10,000 m. The armament consisted of two 20 mm ShVAK cannons and two 7.62 mm ShKAS machine guns. The aircraft had a very sophisticated electric system. Two VI-100 prototypes were built, but with unpressurized cockpits and TK-2 turbochargers. The first VI-100 prototype was flown by Petr M.

Stefanovski on 22 December 1939. The performance – including a speed of 538 km/h at 4,000 m – was far from expected. The supercharger worked well up to an altitude of 5,000 m but at higher altitudes, between 7,000–8,000 m, often failed. The second prototype differed a little from the first one, among other changes having the horizontal stabilizer tips removed from the vertical stabilizer. It was flown by the test pilot A. M. Khripkov and navigator P. I. Perevalov in the spring of 1940. Both prototypes often suffered various failures. The first prototype, after an engine failure, was landed safely with difficulty and much luck by Stefanovski. The second prototype during its second flight caught fire just after take-off, crashed and overturned. The crew survived, but various witnesses on ground were killed. Setting aside these failures and their causes, it was stated that the VI-100 has excellent flight characteristics.

The assessment of potential enemies' air forces development prospects conducted in the USSR revealed that, in the coming years, there would be no need to fight their few high

[1]: The Pe-2 of the commander of the 5. PLB, marked with three horizontal yellow stripes with white outlines painted on the tail and an arrow in similar colours, painted on the forward fuselage. The arrow has a small head and is narrow. The checkerboards are reversed. Soviet airmen pose in front of the aircraft. Sochaczew, July 1945.

[2]: Pe-2 dive bombers of the 5. PLB/1. DLB at a provisional airfield near Sochaczew.

altitude aircraft. It was stated that German Ju 86R and Hs 130 high-altitude strategic reconnaissance aircraft posed no great threat. However, the effectiveness of the new dive bombing tactics, employed by carrier-based US Navy aircraft against enemy ships, was appreciated. Similar bombing tactics were developed in Germany, using the Hs 123 and mass-produced Ju 87 dive bombers. Ju 88 A-1 bombers also had dive bombing capability and the Soviet designers became acquainted with such aircraft, purchased in the USSR. The first dive bomber in the USSR was the Ar-2, designed by A. A. Arkhangelsky, which was a modification of the SB aircraft designed by A. N. Tupolev. The SB design became obsolete, therefore the possibility of further development of the Ar-2 was exhausted. The SPB aircraft, designed by N. N. Polikarpov, five examples of which were built, was superior to the Ar-2 in terms of armament and flight characteristics, but numerous failures occurring during the flight tests meant that the work on it was abandoned. In this aircraft procurement situation, reinforced by the opinion that there was no threat of mass high altitude bomber attack, the high altitude fighter was considered unnecessary. Petlyakov was ordered to redesign the VI-100 into a dive bomber. Petlyakov's team had to accomplish this task within a month and a half.

The first VI-100 prototype was converted into an aircraft renamed PB-100 (*pikinuyushchiy bombardirovshchik*, dive bomber) with a crew of three. Initially the designers intended to retain pressurized cockpits and TK-2 turbochargers. However, in the dive bomber two crew compartments were needed – the forward one for the pilot and the rear one for the navigator (*shturman*) and gunner/wireless operator. Backup flight controls in the navigator's position, in case of the pilot's death or severe injuries, were provided. Retaining the armament in the form of two forward-mounted cannons and two machine guns was initially considered. Initially the PB-100 prototype retained the previous cockpit arrangement and engines with TK-2 turbochargers. However, these features were quickly abandoned as the new aircraft was urgently needed and mass production was planned. The PB-100 prototype was displayed at a parade on 1 May 1940. The production aircraft differed significantly from the prototype. The redesigned cockpit, seating pilot and navigator, was shifted forward in a shortened nose section, thus improving the forward visibility, necessary during dive bombing. In the middle section of the fuselage was the position of gunner/wireless operator and a ventral ShKAS machine gun mount was added. The aircraft was powered by two liquid-cooled (water in the summer and "anti-freeze" coolant in winter) M-105R inline engines, rated at 1,100 hp (without TK-2 turbochargers). The VISh-42 propellers, used in the prototype, were replaced with VISh-61B propellers in production aircraft. In the lengthened engine nacelles small bomb bays for one 100 kg bomb each were added aft of the wheel wells. The height of the vertical stabilizers was increased. About 50 electric motors of five types, rated at 30 – 1,700 W, drove several aircraft systems. The radiator louvres, among others, were electrically actuated and the propeller pitch was controlled electrically. The AP-1 automatic dive controller, bomb bay doors, bomb racks and underwing dive brakes were also electrically actuated, as well as the landing gear, flaps, ailerons, rudders and elevators. The supercharger automatic controllers, pumps and hydraulic system were also electrically driven.

PB-100 production was launched in Factory No. 22, which previously had manufactured Ar-2 bombers. Factory No. 22 was evacuated to Kazan in October 1941. The first aircraft of the first production batch was completed in December 1940. During a parade on 1 May 1941 the 95th Bomber Regiment, commanded by S.A. Pyestov, equipped with Pe-2 flew over Red Square in Moscow. By 22 June 1941 the VVS (*Voyenno-Vozdushnye Sily*, Air Force) of the USSR had received 458 Pe-2 aircraft, but in the western military district on the day of the outbreak of the war there were only 42. In November and December 1941, due to a shortage of materials, a batch of Pe-2 bombers with wooden AV-5 propellers was produced. The aircraft fitted with these propellers were 20–25 km/h slower. Production rate of Pe-2 aircraft, commonly called *Peshka*, gradually increased. A further three factories, Nos. 39, 124 and 125,

[3]: An unidentified Pe-2 crew, probably from the 7. PLB.

[4]: Flaking paint of the checkerboard applied as a wartime marking on a Pe-2 of the 3. PLB. Fronts of the spinners are red.

undertook manufacture of these aircraft. Over the production run, thanks to the introduction of several modifications, the aircraft was constantly improved.

From the 13th batch on the calibre of the armament was increased. Since the Pe-2s often flew without fighter escort, four ShKAS machine guns did not provide sufficient protection against enemy fighters. The forward fixed ShKAS and the one in the ventral MV-2 mount were replaced with 12.7 mm machine guns. In the forward position an UB machine gun was mounted and in the ventral nacelle a UBT.

From the 22nd batch on, the aircraft were powered by improved M-105RA engines, driving WISh-61B propellers.

In the 31st batch the number of windows on the starboard side in the nose glazing was reduced.

Front-line air units urgently needed Pe-2 bombers. The factories, evacuated beyond the Urals, were increasing production output very slowly, with numerous difficulties. There was shortage of labour. Men able to fight had gone to war. Women and children, working in factories 11 hours a day, could not cope with machining of duralumin components. Combat aircrews were reporting deficiencies of design and equipment of the aircraft. These mostly concerned insufficient protection of the crew against enemy fighter attacks. A single ShKAS machine gun in the navigator's TSS-1 mount was insufficient to provide the crew even a chance of defence. In Factory No. 22 an attempt to install two ShKAS guns in this mount was made as early as autumn 1941. There was an attempt to employ the MV-7 turret with Berezin BT large-calibre machine gun, but these changes were not implemented in production aircraft. In Factory No. 22 the new navigator's gun mount, called FT (after *Frontovye Trebovaniya* – front requests) was designed under Selyakov's supervision, using parts of the ventral MV-2 gun mount. It was fitted to a reinforced frame, serving also as cockpit overturn crash frame. The frame was reinforced by two struts on each side of the gun mount and the opening in the fuselage was enlarged. In lieu of the ShKAS gun a UBT gun was installed in the FT mount. Unfortunately this gun position

was not enclosed from the back and in winter the navigator, who manned it, froze in ice cold air stream. To fit the UBT in a stowed position in the fuselage, the capacity of No. 1 fuel tank, mounted just aft of the gun position, was slightly reduced. The first FT gun mounts were installed in some Pe-2 aircraft of the 83rd production batch.

From the 87th batch on the FT gun mounts were installed in all Pe-2 aircraft produced by Factory No. 22. Soon the UBT machine guns began to be installed at front-line airfields in aircraft of earlier production batches. They were installed by both factory teams and ground crew of the bomber units. Pe-2 bombers with FT gun mounts were used in combat with good results near Voronezh. There were cases that German fighter pilots, unaware of these modifications, were shot down while attacking bombers. During the winter of 1941/1942 there were frequent failures of WISh-61B propellers in the dive, due to oil freezing in the cylinders of propeller pitch control mechanisms. The problem was solved by retrofitting the Pe-2 with AV-5 propellers.

According to Russian aviation historians and aircraft technology experts, the Pe-2 variant with VUB-1 gun mount in a rotating turret is in Western (including Polish) literature, and also in Russian publications, was until recently erroneously referred to as Pe-2FT. The incorrect Pe-2FT designation has no relation to the previously used, rearwards-open gun mount referred to as FT. This designation was not used for Pe-2 aircraft in official factory documents. In these documents only the designation Pe-2 with addition of the number of specific production batch was used, e.g. Pe-2 of the 110th batch. Such designation of the Pe-2 aircraft is correct.

Similarly incorrect is the designation "standard Pe-2B", used with reference to Pe-2 aircraft operated in Poland. The Pe-2B aircraft indeed existed, but it was an experimental aircraft with changes introduced by V. M. Myasishchev.

As result of operational experience gained in combat, further changes in production aircraft were introduced. In aircraft of the 83rd production batch changes in nose glazing were introduced. Wide windows in the nose sides were replaced by small

[5]: Pe-2 wearing markings of the commander of the 5. PLB before take-off from Okęcie airfield for the parade over Piłsudski Square in Warsaw on the first anniversary of the end of the Second World War, on 9 May 1946.

5

[6]: *Three mechanics on the wing of Bortnikov's Pe-2. On the starboard side panel of the windscreen three lines, aiding the pilot in dive bombing, are visible. They facilitated visual estimation of the dive angle by aligning the line with the horizon. The aerodynamic compensator (so-called "ear") is visible above the navigator's 12.7 mm UBT machine gun turret.*

[7]: *The lightning on the port side of the Pe-2 of the regiment commander.*

[8]: *A Pe-2 with a small checkerboard on the vertical fin and with lightning flash on the starboard side of the fuselage. The canopy of the gunner-wireless operator's compartment is raised.*

[9]: *Pe-2 aircraft and aircrews of the 7. PLBN before the inspection of the air parade formation by Marshal M. Rola-Żymierski. Okęcie, 9 May 1946.*

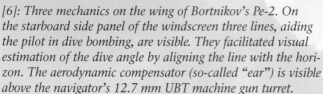

windows. In the round side windows of the gunner/wireless operator position mounts for portable ShKAS machine gun were added. On the rear upper parts of the engine nacelles pairs of hot air vents were added.

From the 105th production batch on, in place of the RPK-2 radio direction finder the newer variant RPK-10 with characteristic loop antenna was installed. The reconnaissance variant Pe-2R was still fitted with RPK-2 radio direction finder.

From 110th production batch on all bombers produced in 1942 were fitted in the *shturman*'s (navigator) VUB-1 gun position with the Berezin UBT large-calibre machine gun, mounted in a rotating turret, designed by Toporov. In order to reduce the force needed to overcome air drag when rotating the machine gun sideways, an aerodynamic compensator with two small fins was added above the turret. The antenna mast was fitted to the rear part of the canopy above the turret. RPK-2 radio direction finder with antenna mounted in a fairing was replaced by more advanced RPK-10 with loop antenna. In the nose glazing two small side windows were retained.

Due to duralumin shortages the Pe-2 aircraft of the 115th production batch had wooden aft fuselage sections. From the 115th batch on the side windows of the nose glazing were removed.

To improve the Pe-2's performance, from the 179th production batch on the M-105RA engines were replaced with the more powerful M-105PF. NII VVS objected to this replacement, predicting that the Pe-2 would be 40–70 km/h slower than the Bf 109. The M-105PF engine was intended for Yak-1, Yak-7 and LaGG-3 fighters and adapted for cannon installation. It was optimized for operation at altitudes of up to 4,000 m. However, the WISh-61B propellers, suitable for the previous engines but unsuitable for the M-105PF, were installed, therefore the Pe-2 had to be operated at lower engine RPM. The M-105PF engines were also retrofitted to Pe-2s of earlier production batches in combat units. Since the cowlings of RA and PF engines differed (the propeller shaft of the PF engine was mounted 60 mm higher than in the RA engine), the older cowlings were cut into halves and new sections were riveted between them.

From the 205th batch on M-105PF engines were installed. In 100 aircraft of this batch individual exhaust stacks were installed instead of exhaust manifolds. To reduce drag generated by the dive brakes, protruding in the stowed position from lower wing surfaces, fairings were added on their edges. The new turret aerodynamic compensator was simplified and had only one balancing surface, the so-called "ear". The antenna mast with Pitot head and air thermometer was moved to the forward canopy frame.

On aircraft of the 211th production batch WISh-61P propellers were installed.

In 1943 a Pe-2 variant with M-82 (later redesignated ASh-82) radial engines, rated at 1,540 hp was built. The 19th aircraft of 31st batch, built in Factory No. 22 (hence its serial number 223119), was redesigned, retrofitted with air-cooled engines and the bomb bays in the engine nacelles were removed. During the next year 135 of this version were built in several batches, including 226, 231, 232 up to 244. Several such aircraft with radial engines were built within various batches along with the aircraft powered by liquid-cooled engines. However, there was a return to manufacture the Pe-2 with M-105PF engines, meanwhile redesignated VK-105PF.

From the 265th batch on the longer range RSB-3bis wireless set began to be installed.

In aircraft of the 271st batch bomb racks of a new design were installed.

On aircraft of the 275th batch an attempt to reinforce the defence of the rear hemisphere was made, by installation of two DAG-10 grenade launchers. Two boxes with five AG-2 grenades were carried in wireless operator/gunner compartment. After being launched the grenade descended on a parachute and exploded in front of the attacking fighter. DAG-10 grenade launchers were also installed in Pe-2 aircraft from earlier batches as early as December 1941 in the 9th Bomber Regiment and in Pe-3 fighters as well.

In aircraft of the 301st batch the upper hatch in gunner/wireless operator compartment was modified.

From the 359th batch on all aircraft had individual exhaust stacks in lieu of exhaust manifolds. The upper hatch of the gunner/wireless operator compartment was fitted with a small windshield tilting forward.

The Pe-2 bombers of 382nd production batch were fitted with an installation facilitating engine startup in winter conditions.

Production of Pe-2 aircraft of all versions, including the Pe-3, continued until 1946. In total 11,247 were built. The Pe-2 was the most produced bomber aircraft in the USSR. In memoirs of veterans of the war, collected by A. Drabkin, the Pe-2 is remembered as underpowered and extremely difficult to fly, especially on take-off and landing. The majority of young, sometimes teenage, pilots flying these bombers had a total flying time of about a dozen or so hours on R-5 and SB aircraft, which were easy to fly. Only the good pilots mastered the difficult *Peshka* – the poorer ones were killed along with their crews at the very beginning, often during the first combat mission. The capability of defending against fighters was poor. The nose machine guns were not used by pilots in such situations. Gunner/ wireless operators, seated on the parachute and ammunition boxes, had no safety belts. They often leaned out of their position, to fire the heavy and difficult to hold ShKAS gun upwards. In one regiment the gun fell out of gunners' hands and fired at friendly aircraft, in another regiment a gunner fell out of the aircraft in dive. During dive bombing runs collisions with their own bombs occurred. Only the pilot had seat harness. The navigator did not and during the dive he had to grip the armoured pilot's seat. The small size of the pilot and navigator (*shturman*) cockpit was very onerous. It limited the navigator's movements. Bent edges of the turret's turntable, in earlier batches not faired over, meant that the navigators could be recognized by threadbare flight suits threadbare, with holes at arm level. In Pe-2 aircraft of later batches the edges of the turntable were faired over.

In October 1944 formation of the 1st Bombardment Division (1. DLB) within the 1st Composite Air Corps began in the USSR. It comprised three bomber aviation regiments (3rd, 4th and 5th BAR). The aforementioned regiments were formed on the basis of three Soviet front-line aviation regiments, previously flying the R-5, Su-2 and Po-2 aircraft. Flight crews and ground personnel of these regiments were initially entirely Soviet. Their gradual and partial replacement with Polish airmen was planned. The Polish airmen, who were to serve in these regiments, came from the draft ordered by the USSR on pre-war Polish territories, liberated from German occupation. They were trained in the USSR in military flying schools. In November 1944 training of Polish pilots began at Engels and the navigators were trained at Chkalov. In June 1944 training of Polish mechanics commenced at Volsk. Conversion from previously operated aircraft to the sophisticated in maintenance and difficult to fly Pe-2 dive bombers required a lot of time and effort of the training crews. Moreover, limited deliveries for a long time did not provide the assigned number of these aircraft in regiments. The full complement of 99 Pe-2 aircraft in the 1st Bombardment Division was attained as late as mid-April 1945. Although training had not been completed, the entire 1st Bombardment Division was deployed to Poland in March/April 1945. The three regiments of the division were stationed at Sochaczew and Sanniki airfields. It was expected that the training program would have been completed in the 1st Bombardment Division by the end of May. All three regiments attained operational readiness on 20 May. The war in Europe ended on 8 May and the Pe-2 bombers with Soviet crews, wearing red stars and Polish checkerboards on their noses, had no opportunity to see combat.

Apart from the 1st Bombardment Division regiments two Pe-2 bombers were in the inventory of 15th Independent Reserve Aviation Regiment (15. SZPL), and the staff flights of Polish Army Air Force, 1st Composite Air Corps and 1st Bombardment Division headquarters had one aircraft assigned to each.

On 1 May 1945 in the inventories of three bomber regiments formed in the USSR: 3rd, 4th and 5th Bomber Regiments, composing the 1st Bombardment Division, were 91 Pe-2 and UPe-2 bombers. The deliveries of Pe-2 and UPe-2 aircraft continued until September 1945. In total 124 aircraft were delivered from the USSR to Poland: 113 Pe-2 bombers and 11 UPe-2 conversion trainers. The delivered Pe-2 aircraft, produced during 1944 and 1945, came from various production batches, 308th to 442nd. Numbers of 106 Pe-2s from 45 production batches are currently known. Delivered UPe-2 aircraft with nine known numbers came from seven batches, 348th to 474th. Due to severe shortage of conversion trainers 20 Pe-2 bombers were converted to

UPe-2 dual control trainers in No. 2 Aircraft Repair Works in Bydgoszcz during 1947–1952. An example of such a conversion is the Pe-2 serial number 20-354. After conversion to the trainer variant this aircraft still had the same number.

Following the end of the war, reorganization of the military, including the air force, began. In peacetime maintaining large armed forces formed during the war was needless and costly. Transition to peacetime status provided for disbandment of two bomber aviation regiments, and retention of one regiment operating front-line Pe-2 bombers.

On 8 June 1945 a Pe-2 of the 4th Bomber Aviation Regiment had an engine failure during a training flight at low altitude. The attempted emergency landing resulted in a crash. The pilot, 2nd Lt Alexei Chistin and navigator, 2nd Lt Mikhail F. Yevgrafovich, were killed. The wireless operator, Sgt Morozov and the passenger, weapons technician Sgt Shemyakin, survived with severe injuries. Nothing else about the accident and its location was revealed, as was customary those days, only the statement that it was a "combat training sortie in accordance with Exercise No. 34 of Bomber Aviation Combat Training Program – 44".

Organization of air parades was to be a test of the high level of combat readiness of the Polish air force and demonstration of its power. The propaganda slogan in No. 2 issue of *Skrzydlata Polska* (Wings of Poland) magazine (July–August 1945) was: "Long live Poland – a mighty aviation state". Pe-2 crews of the 1st Bombardment Division took part in the first air parade and show after the war over Mokotów airfield on 2 September 1945. Nine Pe-2 aircraft, flying in three-ship formations, demonstrated a dive bombing run from an altitude of 3,000 m on a simulated target. The recovery in three-ship formations was made at an altitude of 1,700 m. The audience was most impressed by authentic (as it was thought to be) bombing of targets on the airfield. Powerful explosions seemed to be the results of precise hits on targets placed at short distance (500 m) from the audience... However, flashes and explosions were not results of bombing, but precisely synchronized detonation of previously planted explosives by sappers. It was a reasonable solution, since at that time bombing performed by Pe-2 crews was not always accurate.

[10]: *A portrait photograph of one of nine Pe-2 aircraft, standing in the second row behind Il-2 attack aircraft. The airplane has blue spinner tips, characteristic for the 4. PLB.*

[11]: *The Pe-2 "2" before the air parade over Bydgoszcz on 1 September 1946.*

Pe-2 bombers took part in the Warsaw Victory Parade on 9 May 1946. Before the parade Po-2, UT-2, Pe-2, Il-2, Yak-1 and Yak-9 aircraft with their crews were grouped at Okęcie airfield and reviewed by Marshal of Poland Michał Rola-Żymierski. Nineteen Pe-2 bombers of the 7th Independent Dive Bomber Regiment (7. SPBN) took part for the first time in an air parade over Warsaw. The Pe-2s made a formation flypast and then a bombing display was made by a three-ship flight. Air shows and parades were propaganda demonstrations of the achievements of aviation of the post-war period. The next occasion to organize an air parade and show on 1 September 1946 was the seventh anniversary of the outbreak of the Second World War and 600th anniversary of the city of Bydgoszcz. The Pe-2 bombers of 7. SPBN flew over the Bydgoszcz airfield coming from Fordon in an extended formation and then demonstrated target bombing.

In 1946 the 4th and 5th Bomber Aviation Regiments were disbanded. By the order No. 19 of the Commander-in-Chief of the Polish Army of 29 January 1946 and the order of the commander of Polish Army Aviation of 24 January 1946, the 7th Independent Dive Bomber Regiment (7. SPBN) was formed, based at Leźnica Wielka near Łęczyca. The new unit was formed on the basis of the disbanded 3rd Bomber Aviation Regiment and personnel of the 4th and 5th Bomber Aviation Regiments, as well as the headquarters of the 1st Bombardment Division. Aircraft and air materiel came from the 3rd and 4th Bomber Aviation Regiments. The remaining Pe-2 aircraft were preserved and put in storage. The air component of the 7. SPBN consisted of the staff flight and four air squadrons, comprising three flights. Each squadron was equipped with 10 Pe-2 bombers, one UPe-2 conversion trainer and one Po-2 biplane. The regiment commander, squadron and flight commanders as well as technical and staff personnel were Soviet officers – so the regiment was "properly" manned. In this early period only a few navigators and gunners were Polish. The first group of Polish pilots arrived in Leźnica Wielka on 6 March 1946.

In July 1946 the next Poles joined the regiment – pilots, navigators and gunner/wireless operators. On 21 October 1946 the regiment was reinforced by a group of ten pilots who had graduated from the flying school in the USSR and been promoted to the rank of warrant officer in Dęblin. In November 1946 7. SPBN was expanded by the addition of the Provisional Air Materiel Preservation and Storage Depot in Polska Nowa Wieś near Opole. Hence in December 1946 the inventory of the regi-

[12]: *Four Pe-2 aircraft before the air show on the Aviation Day in Warsaw, 7 September 1947. Three of them took off and demonstrated a dive bombing attack, and one was a spare aircraft.*

ment and depot numbered 108 aircraft – 98 Pe-2, 5 UPe-2 and 5 Po-2. The objective was that, in case of another war threat, the regiment would be the basis for re-establishment of a three regiment bomber division.

In the spring of 1947 the 7. SPBN was reorganized. New establishment of the regiment was introduced on 7 March. From then on the regiment had three air squadrons with 32 Pe-2 bombers, three UPe-2 conversion trainers and three Po-2 biplanes. There was also a staff flight with two UPe-2 aircraft.

During 25/26 March 1947 crews of three flights took part in the removal of the ice jam on the Vistula river near Zakroczym. In the early morning of 25 March, after weather and situation reconnaissance in the jam area, the regiment commander, Lt Col. Szczepan Ścibior, led the first flight to the Vistula river, dropping two FAB-250 and two FAB-100 bombs on the front of the ice jam. In total 26 sorties in nine Pe-2 aircraft were flown during this operation. About 15 tonnes of bombs – 18 FAB-250 and 108 FAB-100 – were dropped on the jam. The commander of the Air Force, Gen. Fyodor Polynin, observed the beginning of the operation, circling in his Airacobra "01" over the jam and later assessed the actions of the regiment's airmen highly. During 11–21 April 1947 the regiment was moved from Leźnica Wielka air base to Ławica airfield in Poznań. It was a great logistic effort. The redeployment of the entire unit required two railway transports with 100 wagons in total. The aircraft were ferried to the new base in three batches (ten Pe-2 aircraft on 12 April, during the next two days the remaining aircraft, 23 Pe-2s and four Po-2s, were ferried). From mid-April flying continued at Ławica airfield. Despite the complex operation of the redeployment of the entire regiment, in April a flight time of 131 hours and 16 minutes was amassed, which was 164% of the plan. During intense flying in May a few failures and an air accident took place. Since the beginning of 1947 there was increasingly severe shortages of spare parts and engines for Pe-2 aircraft, because the USSR did not supply them as it was obliged to. It made systematic training impossible and caused increas-

[13-15]: Three photographs of Pe-2 aircraft with large checkerboards on the nose, applied during the war. The spinners are red. Dęblin 1946.

[16]: *Pe-2 bombers of the Officer Flying School's 4th Squadron, wearing wartime paint scheme with checkerboards on the noses, are visible in the background behind the Yak-9V aircraft. Dęblin, summer of 1946.*

ingly more frequent and severe failures. On 13 May an UPe-2, piloted by Lt Col. Ścibior, force landed due to engine failure. On 17 May 1st Lt Kilachov (a Soviet officer) also made a forced belly landing in an UPe-2 due to loss of terrain orientation.

On 28 May 1947 the crew of 2nd Lt Bogusław Gorbaszewicz had an accident on take-off for a training flight from Ławica airfield. At an altitude of about 100 m both engines lost power. The pilot decided to land straight ahead in a large field behind a forest, but failed to avoid collision with a large, lone pine tree. The force of the collision was so great that, despite its ruggedness, the aircraft broke into pieces. The engines, broken fuselage, wings and empennage were scattered over a large area. Only the pilot and navigator's compartment and part of the gunner/wireless operator's compartment remained near the tree and were only slightly damaged. The unconscious airmen, with numerous injuries, were taken to hospital. Fate was quite kind on them. The pilot returned to flying, the navigator, 2nd Lt Antoni Wawryn, regained his health but did not return to aviation. The gunner/wireless operator had a spine injury and did not fully recover. All these failures and crash affected the aircrew morale badly. A recess in flying, aircraft technical inspections and additional training were ordered. Six Pe-2 crews of 7. SPBN took part in a central, several days long, training course for flight leaders organized in June at Bydgoszcz airfield. During the return flight to Ławica airfield an accident took place, fortunately without tragic results. A Pe-2 flown by 1st Lt Jerzy Gindrych crashed on landing. The crew was uninjured, but the aircraft was written off.

In 1948 the 7. SPN was renamed 7th Dive Bomber Regiment (7. PBN). The new name was for the first time used in the order of the Commander of the Air Force of 8 January 1948. At the beginning of the year a flight of Pe-2 aircraft was tasked with target towing during anti-aircraft artillery exercises at Wicko Morskie gunnery range. This flight was operationally subordinated to Aerial Defence Command.

Pe-2 bombers that had been operated during the war were still the regiment's main equipment, therefore their wear was very heavy. The number of Pe-2 aircraft was reduced on 9 October 1948. On that day three were transferred to the Naval Air Squadron, formed at Wicko Morskie. After a few weeks one UPe-2 was also transferred to Wicko from the Poznań regiment.

In the middle of September 1948 Air Force Staff ordered the participation of four flights of Pe-2 aircraft in the first manoeuvres after the war. The selected crews were to operate from a provisional airfield in Krzewica, near Międzyrzecz Podlaski. The flight from the 1st squadron was led by 2nd Lt Kazimierz Wierzbicki with navigator 2nd Lt Bolesław Duźniak and gunner/wireless operator W/O Waldemar Lipiński. The second crew comprised 2nd Lt Edward Szafrański (pilot) and 2nd Lt Roman Biała (navigator). The third crew comprised 2nd Lt Henryk Jabłoński (pilot), 2nd Lt Julian Rydlicki (navigator) and S/Sgt Leon Iwanow. In the exercise a flight of aircraft piloted by Soviet officers also took part, acting as advisors to the Polish squadron commanders: First Lieutenants Usov, Polkanov and Yemielin. The ferry flight from Ławica to the provisional airfield was made in formation with three aircraft flying line astern at an altitude of 500–700 m. The aircraft parked at the provisional airfield were camouflaged with nets and tree branches. The exercise began on 15 September. The short airstrip was quite soft and the aircraft took off individually. Sorties to Jagodne bombing range were flown with fighter escort. The bombs were dropped on the range in two runs, with simulated AAA fire.

During the exercise an accident occurred on 23 September. The crew of Pe-2 piloted by 2nd Lt E. Szafrański could not drop all its bombs on the range and two FAB-100 bombs remained hung up in the bomb bay. Two attempts to drop them with unarmed fuses failed. Due to the fact that fuel was running out, the pilot decided to make a belly landing in a field near the Vistula river. The bombs did not fall out of the racks during the belly landing and remained unexploded. The forced wheels-up landing with

200 kg bomb load ended safely. The crew remained unscathed and the airplane was only slightly damaged.

On 20 October 1948 an UPe-2 was damaged during a training flight.

In 1949, due to increasingly more frequent failures of Pe-2 aircraft, the number of high angle dive bombing sorties was greatly reduced.

On 17 May 1949 the Pe-2 "22" of the regiment's third squadron crashed during a flight in the traffic pattern. After take-from Leźnica air base and a turn to the crosswind leg the pilot, W/O Stefan Czapla, lowered the landing gear at an altitude of 400 m. He made the next turn to the downwind leg with lowered landing gear too sharply, with a 70-degree bank. The aircraft stalled and hit the ground. The pilot and navigator, Staff Sgt/Officer Cadet Roman Kułak, were killed and the gunner/wireless operator, Cpl Stefan Dąsal, was severely injured.

According to Col. Tadeusz Dalecki, another emergency landing of a Pe-2 in 7. PBN took place. This event was described in this author's book *Gościnne niebo* ("Hospitable sky") in 1977. Probably it was the only case of an emergency rough field landing of a Pe-2 with lowered landing gear. One can

imagine what flying the Pe-2 and the "rescue effort" looked like those days. Here is the shortened account of this flight and landing. The pilot, 2nd Lt Edward Mataczun, was tasked by the regiment's commander (then Lt Col. Bortnikov) with bombing the target at Biedrusko bombing range, followed by a cross-country flight over a pre-ordered route. The pilot was to report on the radio the bomb drop and his position at every turning point. The navigator on this sortie was 2nd Lt Tadeusz Piechurowski. The Pe-2 flew a circuit over the airfield and after a four-minute flight the bombs were dropped on the target – a line of old tanks, brought from various battlefields to Biedrusko. Having sent the report to the command post after the bomb drop the crew proceeded to the second part of the task, flying at an altitude of 1,500 m. The Pe-2 crossed the railway line from Września to Jarocin, then the Warta river near Czeszewo and flying over the Prosna river arrived over Kalisz, where it turned, heading for Jarocin. When the aircraft passed Jarocin, there was a violent shock and vibration. The pilot, known in the regiment for his sense of humour and tendency to burst into uncontrolled laughter even in presence of superiors, told himself, assessing the situation: "*Look out Eddie – there may be a mess in a moment*". After a while the situation repeated. The port engine quit. The pilot countered the yaw with the right rudder and applied full throttle to the starboard engine. He knew that he would not make it to base on one engine. He switched the damaged engine off and feathered its propeller. The aircraft was losing altitude and 2nd Lt Mataczun shouted to the navigator: "*Teddy! Look for a landing ground*". The navigator lost his mind and instead of looking for a landing ground he embraced the pilot's chest, pressing it against the backrest. He forgot that he should have done it on the round out. The emergency landing drill read as follows: "*When the Pe-2 is about to make an emergency landing, the pilot must land the aircraft with landing gear up and the navigator must hold*

[17]: Red "7" digit with white outline on a Peshka. Officer cadet Ryszard Szmitkowski, training on the Il-2 attack aircraft, is posing for the photograph. Dęblin 1945/46.

[18]: Cadets of the Officer Flying School in Dęblin having a break in training flights. Eight Pe-2 aircraft of the school's inventory are visible in the background.

[19]: *A staged photo of the airmen of the 22ⁿᵈ Bomber Group of the Officer Flying School. Dęblin 1947.*

[20]: *Fragment of the tail fin of a Pe-2 "01", standing behind Gen. F. Polynin's Airacobra, also numbered "01". This number with the first digit "0" on a Pe-2 indicates an aircraft assigned to one of executive flights of the Air Force HQ or a bomber division HQ.*

the pilot to prevent him from hitting his head against the sight". The navigator's grasp was so strong that the pilot was not able to free himself and fly the airplane, which could have gone into spin. With only one engine running and at such a low altitude there was no chance to recover. With great effort the pilot eventually managed to free himself from the overpowering grasp of the astounded navigator. When the aircraft was flying at an altitude of 300 m over Środa Wielkopolska, the radio communication cut off. Beside the railroad, over which the Pe-2 flew at low altitude, was a meadow with grazing cows and haystacks. The pilot did not want to make a belly landing, to save the engines and propellers. He decided to land on his wheels. He flew over a drainage ditch and escaping cows. The airplane rolled near a haystack and stopped short of the next drainage ditch. The crew and airplane survived. The navigator walked to Środa Wielkopolska to phone the regiment commander and tell him about the emergency landing, while the pilot and gunner stayed with the airplane. Children from a nearby house brought a jug of milk and apples. After some time a Po-2 with the regiment commander and squadron technical officer arrived and landed near the Pe-2. The pilot's claim that the magnetos failed was confirmed – the exhaust pipes were wet streaks of gasoline. Fortunately the aircraft did not catch fire. "Sometimes it happens" chuckled the pilot. 2ⁿᵈ Lt Mataczun received Lt Col. Bortnikov's commendation on the spot and flew with him to Ławica air base in the Po-2. The navigator returned to Poznań by train. Two days later the squadron commander, Maj. Imyelin, ferried the repaired Pe-2 back to base. Unfortunately the author describing the event did not provide the date of 2ⁿᵈ Lt Mataczun's emergency landing.

In 1949 the 7. PBN lost a Pe-2 aircraft piloted by 2ⁿᵈ Lt Zygmunt Pędzisz. After a botched hard landing at Ławica airfield the airplane caught fire. The emergency canopy jettisoning attempt failed because drying paint, applied by the mechanics making up the coating defects, jammed the wires releasing the canopy catches. The pilot and navigator managed to escape the burning airplane, squeezing through open cockpit windows. The gunner/wireless operator also managed to abandon the aircraft. Lt Col Bortnikov repeatedly reproached the pilot for burning the aircraft during regimental briefings (according to Kazimierz Gawron's account).

Unreliable, weary Pe-2 aircraft eventually gained the notoriety of "flying coffins". The bad situation with equipment at that time can be shown by the refusal to fly a Pe-2 by the commander of the 2ⁿᵈ Squadron, Capt. Stanisław Turczyński. He could afford it only because he was a Soviet officer. Moreover,

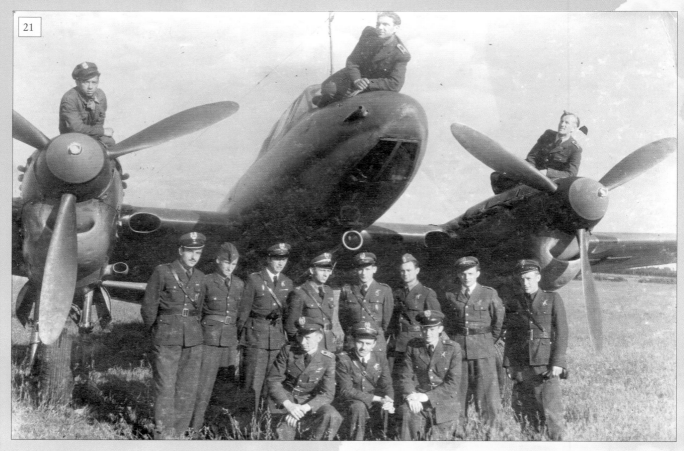

[21]: Aircrews of the 7. SPLBN posing on and in front of a Pe-2 aircraft. Standing third from left is 2nd Lt Kazimierz Wierzbicki. The aircraft was previously operated by the 4. PLB, hence the blue spinner tips.

the condition of 7. PBN was deteriorating not only because of the lack of engine and spare parts supplies, but also due to formation of new units using its personnel and aircraft. On 10 October 1949 eight Tu-2S bombers were delivered to the 7. PBN, but it did not change the situation of the regiment much, since the primary type was still the Pe-2. During February-May 1950 several airmen were transferred from the 7. PBN to newly-formed Long Range Reconnaissance Squadron (including Capt. S. Turczyński, who was appointed commander of the 30th Naval Air Regiment). The operation of eight Tu-2 aircraft by 7. PBN did not last long because, along with the departing aircrews, the regiment's inventory was reduced by two Tu-2S aircraft and the only UTu-2, which was transferred to the naval squadron.

At the end of 1950/early 1951 further changes in the post-war organization of the Air Force were introduced. It was caused among other things by the Korean War, which could have evolved into a world conflict. The 15th Bombardment Division was established by the order of 7 April 1950 from the cadre of the 7th Bomber Aviation Regiment based at Malbork.

On 1 May 1950 the participation of the regiment's aircraft in the air parade over Warsaw was planned. The parade formation was assembled at Kroczewo airfield near Zakroczym. There the Pe-2 and all the regiment's Tu-2S aircraft were based during the preparations and training for the parade. For the summer training during 16 May-7 June 1950 the regiment's aircraft were deployed to the other Poznań air base, Krzesiny. Among other exercises bombing was practiced at Biedrusko range near Poznań. On 11 July 1950 the regiment obtained

a new organizational structure and two months later was renamed 7th Bomber Aviation Regiment (7. PLB). For the exercise at the end of the summer 7. PLB was deployed to Leźnica Wielka air base.

Operating from this base the entire regiment performed bombing at a range near Dęblin. The first to drop bombs were the crews of the Tu-2S aircraft, which had better navigation equipment than weary Pe-2 bombers. During the flight to the range one Pe-2 crew had to jettison unarmed bombs and make an emergency belly landing due to engine failure. The aircraft was damaged, but the crew survived. After more than a three years long stay at Ławica air base the 7. PLB was redeployed to Malbork during 20–24 October 1950. At Ławica air base only the component detached from the 3rd Squadron of 7. PLB with Pe-2 aircraft remained, as the core for forming a squadron of the future 21st Reconnaissance Aviation Regiment. Severe shortages of spare parts and wear of Pe-2 aircraft meant that on 17 April 1951 in the inventory of 7. PLB were 29 airplanes of various types, including 14 Pe-2, 2 UPe-2, 5 Tu-2S, 1 UTB-2 and 7 Po-2.

On 19 May 1951 a Pe-2 piloted by 2nd Lt Janusz Łukaszewicz took off from Malbork air base. 2nd Lt Henryk Droździk was the navigator. The crew's task was to make a cross-country flight, take photographs of Iława railway station and then drop four 75 kg bombs on target at a bombing range. Short of Iława, at an altitude of 2,000 m, the gunner noticed a leak from the starboard engine. It turned out soon that the coolant from the starboard engine was leaking. The pointer of the coolant

[22]: *Pe-2 aircraft of the 7. SPLBN a few days before the redeployment from Leźnica Wielka to Ławica. 2ⁿᵈ Lt Jan Wilkosz (left) is talking to a superior. Leźnica Wielka, April 1947.*

[23]: *2ⁿᵈ Lt Kazimierz Wierzbicki (left) and 1ˢᵗ Lt Tadeusz Bacdorf standing next to a Pe-2 bomber, Leźnica Wielka 1947.*

[24]: *1ˢᵗ Lt Wierzbicki (center) with his crew before a sortie.*

temperature gauge soon passed the red sector and stopped at the end of the scale. The smell of hot oil filled the cockpit. The pilot decided to return to base. He made a left turn, taking a reverse course. The engine started to lose RPM, which had to be reduced to idle. Despite almost maximum RPM of the working engine, level flight was impossible and the aircraft was losing altitude. Unfortunately, this was a common feature of all Pe-2 bombers – level flight on one engine without losing altitude was impossible. Depending on the pilot's skills and luck the two options were a forced landing or crash. There was only the hope that the engine would not seize and that the port engine, working at maximum RPM, would hold out to the end of the flight. The navigator calculated that if the sink rate remained unchanged, the airplane would probably make it back to base with 200 m altitude reserve. The pilot did not take jettisoning bombs, even unarmed, into consideration since the terrain beneath the aircraft was built-up and populated. However, the aircraft made it to Malbork air base and slowly turning to port on the one working engine, aligned with the runway centreline. At an altitude of 180 m the pilot lowered the landing gear. When the wheels touched the runway the starboard engine stopped. The pilot switched off both engines and the airplane veered off the runway and stopped on the grass. The crew and airplane survived.

On 22 July 1951 Pe-2s again took part in the air parade over Warsaw. They flew in formation over Marszałkowska Street and Bankowy Square, where the parade stand stood. The parade took place on the occasion of the communist holiday of 22 July and unveiling of the monument of the Bolshevik Felix Dzerzhinsky and the square on which the monument stood was named after him.

By the Ministry of Defence orders of April and the order of the commander of the 15th Bombardment Division of 1 August 1951, air and ground crews were detached from 7. PLB to form the 33. PLB, the complement of which was to comprise only two squadrons. The main equipment of the newly-formed regiment were weary Pe-2 bombers.

In the morning hours of 23 September 1951, during a joint exercise with the Navy a Pe-2 crewed by 2nd Lt Zdzisław Piatczyc (pilot), 2nd Lt Jerzy Janiak (navigator) and Sgt Kazimierz Łosicki (gunner/wireless operator) took part. A flight of six Pe-2 aircraft, led by Capt. Eugeniusz Waszyrowski, took off from Ławica air base, tasked with a making a mock bombing raid on Świnoujście harbour. When the formation crossed the Noteć river the weather conditions deteriorated. The flight leader ordered to abort the mission and the group turned to return to base. During this manoeuver 2nd Lt Piatczyc failed to keep in formation, separated from the rest and lost spatial orientation in clouds. The pilot and navigator had no experience in flying in low visibility conditions. The aircraft hit the ground near Tuczno, in the vicinity of Jastrowie. The entire crew were killed.

On 28 November 1951 in the inventory of the re-formed 7th BR were only 21 aircraft of various types, including 11 Pe-2 bombers, 3 UPe-2, 4 Tu-2, 1 UTB-2 and 2 Po-2.

Soon in the 15th Bombardment Division formation of the next, third bomber regiment, equipped with Pe-2 aircraft, began. The command of the 15th Bombardment Division was ordered by the MoD to form the 35th Bomber Aviation Regiment at Bydgoszcz airbase by 1 December 1952. Its intended base was Inowrocław. During the period of formation of new bomber regiments and detaching aircraft and personnel for them from 7. PLB, owing to force of circumstances this regiment suffered

[25]: Pe-2 aircraft of the 2nd Squadron of 7. SPLBN redeployed from Leźnica Wielka, standing on the concrete apron after the arrival at Ławica airfield, April 1947.

[26]: Gunner/wireless operators of the 7. SPLBN. Forward sections of the airplane's spinners are yellow.

severe personnel and equipment shortage. The 7.PLB had only 15 pilots at that time, including 11 with little experience (who had graduated in 1950–1952). The number of aircraft in the inventory diminished. On 21 April 1952 the regiment had 26 aircraft, including 14 Pe-2, 3 UPe-2 and 4 Tu-2S, one UTB-2 and 4 Po-2.

The new 35. PLB had nine aircraft in its inventory, including seven old, weary Pe-2s, one UPe-2 and one Po-2. Later three Tu-2S, three Pe-2, one UPe-2 and one Po-2 were transferred from the inventories of 7. PLB and 33. PLB. The inventory of 35. PLB increased to 17 aircraft. These combat aircraft were to be operated by the unit until planned re-equipment of the regiment with jet-powered Il-28 bombers. Piston-powered bombers were operated by 35. PLB until 1954. At that time the regiment was based at Przasnysz and there the Pe-2 aircraft were left, intended for scrapping. Two Tu-2S aircraft were transferred to a target towing flight based at Świdwin and the Po-2s were transferred to Modlin. In May 1954 the 35. PLB was redeployed to Modlin, where it received the first two Il-28 jet bombers on 6 June.

Another unit equipped with Pe-2 aircraft was the Reconnaissance Aviation Squadron, formed in 1950 at Ławica air base in Poznań. The squadron was again formed on the basis of 7. PLB. The squadron received 9 Pe-2, one UPe-2 and one Po-2 aircraft, transferred from 7. PLB. Capt. A. Dubovoy, a Soviet officer, was appointed as the squadron commander. In the squadron, formation of which began in October, flying training was commenced on 1 December 1950.

Even during the practical training period a crash occurred in the squadron on 16 January 1951. The Pe-2, serial number 11-369, tail number "11", piloted by 2nd Lt Marian Terpliwy, with the navigator, W/O Kazimierz Knobel and gunner/wireless operator Sgt Witold Domański, flying in the circuit pattern lost speed (probably due to engine failure). It went into flat, right-hand spin and hit the ground. The committee investigating the crash stated that it was caused by insufficient pilot's skills in maintaining aircraft's speed and violation of rules contained in the Pe-2's flying manual. During this period such committees usually stated pilot error, disregarding technical reasons, concerning aircraft made in the USSR.

In April 1951 formation of the 21st Reconnaissance Aviation Regiment (21. PLZ) on the basis of the existing squadron began. After the unit had been supplied with combat aircraft the 3rd and 4th Long Range Reconnaissance Squadrons and staff flight were established. In June, after redeployment to Kroczewo airfield near Modlin, one squadron for the first time took part in joint five-day exercises with army units. Sorties were flown to the Bydgoszcz-Grudziądz-Gdańsk line. The crews flew individual and two-ship sorties for visual and photographic reconnaissance of troop concentrations. Area photographing and a more difficult task, taking oblique photographs of the forward line of enemy defences, were also practised. Another test of the skills of the crews of 21. PLZ was the participation of one Pe-2 squadron in an air parade over Warsaw. For the period of preparation for the parade the assigned squadron with maintenance crew was redeployed from Ławica to Modlin air

[27-28]: *A freshly painted* Peshka *without tail number, put on display on the Aviation Day, 5 September 1948. Four FAB-250 bombs are suspended on the external racks under the wing centre section. A plaque with the caption "Pe-2 bomber aircraft" hangs on the direction finder loop antenna.*

[29]: *Cadets of the Officer Flying School during training activities on a Pe-2 wearing a wartime camouflage pattern, Dęblin 1948.*

base, where the aircraft taking part in the parade were grouped. During autumn inspection of the unit the evaluation of the unit's combat capabilities was area photography of assigned sectors in two runs and bombing of a target with series of three bombs at Biedrusko range.

On 10 June 1952 a crash of Pe-2 serial number 14-353 and tail number "6" occurred in 21. PLZ. Flying in the circuit pattern over Starołęka in Poznań, the crew reported starboard engine failure. Soon the port engine cut out too. To avoid crashing in downtown Poznań the pilot turned east, trying to land in an unpopulated area. However, he was not able to do it and the aircraft crashed in the city center, at the intersection of Droga Dębińska-Marchlewskiego (now Królowej Jadwigi)-Garbary streets. The entire crew, W/O Zdzisław Lara (pilot), W/O Stanisław Kuć (nawigator) and Cpl Józef Bednarek (gunner/wireless operator) were killed. Fuel and ammunition exploded. Six people in the street were killed and a further ten were injured. The crash was kept secret. The committee, headed by Soviet General Ivan Turkiel, forged the description of the course of the flight and stated that "*the probable cause of the crash was pilot error, consisting in execution of the final turn in the wrong place and at wrong altitude*". After the crash the engines of all Pe-2 aircraft in the regiment were checked, four were repaired without being removed from the airplanes and seven engine blocks were replaced.

During 15 May – 14 June 1952 regiment crews flew sorties on Pe-2 aircraft during the making of the film *Soldier of Victory*.

In early spring of 1953 another accident of a Pe-2 occurred. The crew commanded by 2nd Lt Gruszczyński, after having accomplished gunnery exercise over the range, lost orientation and made an emergency landing near Częstochowa. A month later the crew of 2nd Lt Niewiadomski made an emergency landing due to fuel pump failure. In June the situation with equipment improved – the regiment received three Tu-2S and one UTB-2 aircraft. Pe-2s remained in service in 21. PLZ till 1954.

The Military Flying School at Dęblin on 1 May 1945 had 12 Pe-2 bombers in its inventory. In early 1946 the 1st Independent Aviation Training Regiment based at Radom was disbanded and its subunits were incorporated into the Military Flying School at Dęblin. Pe-2 pilots were trained in the 5th Squadron. In 1946 the Pe-2 inventory was expanded by several UPe-2 trainers. During the training on Pe-2 and UPe-2 aircraft eleven airmen were killed in four crashes. One Pe-2 and three UPe-2 trainers were lost.

On 31 October 1947 UPe-2, tail number "0." (the other digit of the number, preceded by 0 is invisible on the photograph of the wreck) crashed. The crew from the training squadron, Lt Col. Boris Bortkievich (a Soviet) officer, W/O Jan Kramek and W/O Jan Lewandowski, was flying the circuit pattern over Dęblin airfield. After the turn onto finals at a height of 100 m the port flap groups failed to extend. The aircraft rapidly changed direction flight, went into a spin and crashed. The entire crew were killed.

The second crash occurred on 9 June 1950 on take-off of a Pe-2 for an aerial gunnery training sortie. During the take-off run the pilot did not raise aircraft's tail, causing a premature lift-off and change of direction of the take-off. At a distance of 1,700 m from the lift-off point the aircraft hit a building's roof, hit the ground and burned. The entire crew, 2nd Lt Lucjan

Duda (pilot), W/O Kazimierz Rosiński (navigator) and trainee gunner/wireless operator Stanisław Mista, were killed.

A tragic month in the history of the Dęblin school was July 1952, during which two crashes occurred. The training squadron was operating from a provisional airfield at Sochaczew. The UPe-2 tail number "10" had an in-flight engine failure. On approach to emergency landing the pilot veered off course to avoid collision with trees and the aircraft hit the ground with one wing and crashed. The instructor pilot, 2nd Lt Tadeusz Bartosiak, the trainee pilot, Pvt Officer Cadet Józef Mirecki, technician W/O Tadeusz Borowiecki and gunner/wireless operator, Cpl Zdzisław Chochół, were killed. The second crash occurred on 23 July. The pilot of UPe-2 tail number "2" was making his sixth solo flight in the circuit pattern. He lost speed and the aircraft stalled, went into spin and crashed 6.5 km from Sochaczew airfield. The entire crew, Sgt Officer Cadet Kazimierz Szaliński (pilot), PFC Officer Cadet Tadeusz Kikoła (navigator) and Sgt Jan Zaręba (gunner/wireless operator), were killed.

The first naval air unit equipped with the Pe-2 was the Naval Air Squadron. This squadron was established by the organizational order of the Minister of Defence no. 030/org of 28 February 1948. The order required the commander of the Air Force to form the Naval Air Squadron. Initially the location was Poznań, but by the decision of the MoD No. 122 of 21 March 1948 the location was changed from Poznań to Ustka. On 9 October 1948 three Pe-2 aircraft were ferried from 7. PBN to Ustka. They were assigned to the bomber-reconnaissance flight. These were war-weary aircraft. Their VK-105PF engines had 50% of their total time expired. The Pe-2 aircraft had their flight control systems weakened by intense wartime service, hence diving was prohibited. They could not be used as dive bombers, though they still could be used as horizontal bombers. Thanks to AFA cameras installed in the fuselage they were capable of performing reconnaissance missions. The ceremonial handover of the squadron formed by the Air Force Command to the Naval Command took place on 18 October 1948 at Wicko Morskie airfield. After several weeks one UPe-2 trainer, necessary for pilot and navigator training in flying over the sea, was delivered from 7. PBN to Wicko Morskie. It was assigned to the bomber-reconnaissance flight. On 18 October 1948 in the inventory of the Independent Naval Air Squadron were three Pe-2 aircraft, serial numbers 4-363, 6-365 and 8-401. The single UPe-2 aircraft, added to the inventory later, had the serial number 4-348 and tail number S3. By the order of 22 November 1949 the Minister of Defence required the Commander-in-chief of the Navy to disband the Naval Air Squadron by 25 March 1950 and form on its basis the 30th Naval Aviation Regiment (30. PL MW), the 50th Naval Airfield Maintenance Battalion (50. BOL MW) and Naval Aviation Training Company. The aforementioned order required the CinC of the Navy to form a Long Range Reconnaissance Squadron (on the basis of the bombardment and reconnaissance flight of the disbanded Naval Air Squadron), train it in 7. PBN based at Ławica and transfer the newly formed squadron to the 30. PL MW. Słupsk air base was selected as the place of formation and base of 30. PL MW. LCdr Stanisław Turczyński (a Soviet officer) was appointed the commander of 30. PL MW. As early as 7 February 1950 the first muster of the personnel of 30. PL MW, 50. BOL MW and Naval Aviation Training Squadron took place and LCdr S.

[31]: The Pe-2 "15" as a backdrop of the photograph of Officer Flying School cadets in Dęblin in 1948. Standing first from left is Sgt Officer Cadet Kazimierz Gawron.

[30]: In this photograph, taken at Ławica airfield in 1949, the base of the windshield frame with open lock and the cockpit inlet of the wire antenna of RSBF-5 radio are visible.

[32-33]:The Air Force commander hands over the Naval Air Squadron with a detachment of Pe-2 aircraft to the commander of the Navy. The aircraft have lower sections of the tail fins and spinners with markings worn during their service in the 7. SPLBN. Wicko Morskie, 18 October 1948.

[34]: *An unidentified Pe-2 and UT-2 in a 1949 photograph.*

Turczyński reported readiness for duty. The first familiarisation flight over the sea was made by the Long Range Reconnaissance Squadron of 30. PL MW on 8 March 1950. Training sorties on UPe-2 were commenced on 21 March. Pe-2 crews practised cross-country, circuit pattern and formation flying. In April formation flying was intensely practised before the parade scheduled for 1 May.

On 14 April 1950 the UPe-2 tail number "S3" was damaged during a flying technique check sortie. The crew comprised the instructor pilot, 1st Lt Stanisław Gajewski, the examined pilot 2nd Lt Teodor Figiel and navigator W/O Jacek Łęski. The aircraft, flying too low before touchdown, hit the embankment of a transverse road on approach. The tailwheel ripped off and bounced, followed by the airplane ploughing the airfield turf with the wheel strut. The crew was unhurt but the lack of the regiment's only trainer aircraft made the evaluation of pilots' flying skills before the forthcoming parade rather difficult. However, the ground crews managed to partly repair the damaged aircraft, which was then sent to No. 2 Military Aircraft Repair Facility in Bydgoszcz.

After the deployment to Kroczewo airfield near Zakroczym cross-country flying in three-ship formations was practised. The first and successful evaluation of the capabilities of the regiment's crews was the participation in the central parade on 1 May in Warsaw. Five days later Pe-2 crews commenced gunnery, bombing and reconnaissance training sorties. Similar tasks were conducted in June.

After the repair in Bydgoszcz the UPe-2 tail number "S3" returned to the unit on 29 June 1950. It was collected by the crew comprising LTJG Edward Mataczun (pilot), Ens. Kazimierz Gawron (navigator), Petty Officer 3rd Class Edward Kuper (gunner/wireless operator) and Chief Petty Officer Józef Jagodziński (technician), who took the seat in instructor's cockpit. The cloud base was low on that day, which prevented flying at high altitude. The pilot, known for his excellent flying skills, landed the UPe-2 at the home base after a 49-minute long low-level flight.

In August joint exercises with ships commenced. In Bay of Gdańsk area the Pe-2 crews practised gunnery and bombing a moving target, towed by ships between Mikoszewo and Hel. Such a target was bombed with LBC-50 concrete bombs. These bombs had AMA impact fuses. A plume of smoke was visible at the point of the bomb impact instead of detonation. The Bay of Puck was used as a bombing range and the fixed target was the wreck of the Polish ship ORP *Gryf*, sunk in September 1939, lying in the shallows. The wreck was clearly visible from the air and was used as a bombing and gunnery

target. As of 24 November 1950 in the inventory of the Long Range Reconnaissance Squadron of 30. PL MW were seven Pe-2 and one UPe-2 aircraft. Pe-2 aircraft coming from six production batches had following serial and tail numbers: 6-364 tail number "6", 6-365 tail number "4", 8-401 tail number "7", 13 – 357 tail number "3", 16-383 tail number "5", 17-355 tail number "6" and 18-400 tail number "1". The UPe-2 trainer had the serial number 4-348 and tail number "S3". One Pe-2 aircraft was assigned to the squadron commander. The remaining bombers were assigned to the first and second flight, three to each. (Moreover, the Long Range Reconnaissance Squadron had one Tu-2S and one dual control trainer UTu-2 and the third Tu-2 was assigned to the staff flight). In April 1951 one Pe-2 aircraft was sent for major overhaul.

In May 1951 30. PL MW was deployed to Gdynia – Babie Doły air base, which was vacant after the departure of the 3rd Fighter Aviation Regiment. On Pe-2 departed Słupsk – Redzikowo air base with the air component of Long Range Reconnaissance Squadron.

In early 1952 the squadron was reinforced with new Pe-2 crews, usually second lieutenants and warrant officers.

On 29 June 1952 the Pe-2 aircraft from the Long Range Reconnaissance Squadron took part in the air parade on the occasion of the Navy Day. Prior to the parade formation flying with timing of the flypast over the ships participating in the parade was practised. The air component was led by Po-2 aircraft carrying white and red flags attached to poles. The Long Range Reconnaissance Squadron deployed a flight of Pe-2 aircraft. The air component was ended by Tu-2 aircraft. The flypast over the ships was made twice. First the aircraft flew in formations of three and in the second flypast the same aircraft flew in line astern formation. It was a propaganda action, disguising the real strength of the naval aviation. It was intended to make an impression of great power of the actually very small naval aviation.

On 15 July 1952 the Pe-2 and Tu-2 aircraft of the Long Range Reconnaissance Squadron were deployed to Wrzeszcz airfield. The home base was temporarily vacated to enable renovation of some premises, modernization and lengthening of the runway, pointing towards the Bay of Puck. Due to the hot summer, causing overheating of Pe-2 and Il-10 aircraft engines, on the flying days training commenced in the early morning hours. The intensity of combat training sorties flown in semi-field conditions from Wrzeszcz airfield was considerable. The return of the entire unit from Wrzeszcz to Babie Doły air base took place on 30 August 1952.

[35]: Open cockpit hatch with the step extended. The serial number 2-356 (second airplane of 356th production batch) is visible on the wing centre section's leading edge. The loop antenna RPK-O-10 direction finder is mounted next to the lower aft section of the nose glazing.

[36]: An unidentified crew in front of a Pe-2 aircraft. The cockpit hatch is open, but the extendable step is stowed.

[37]: The commander of the 7. SPLBN, Col. Szczepan Ścibior, in flight suit and with flying helmet, standing against a background of Pe-2 aircraft, accompanied by Soviet officers serving in the regiment. Leźnica Wielka airfield near Łęczyca.

[38]: Capt. Wierzbicki, 2nd Lt Żak (center) and 2nd Lt Królikowski (with a map case) standing next to a Pe-2 at Malbork airfield, spring 1951.

[39]: A Pe-2 crew posing for a photograph, The spinner is two-colour. The tail fin of the aircraft in the background has the rudder repainted and the lower section of the vertical stabilizer was still probably red. Malbork 1951.

40

41

[40-42]: A series of three staged photos in front of a Pe-2 aircraft, showing the mechanics at work, crew chief report and the aircrew prior to a sortie. The spinners are two-colour (red/white?). The aircraft visible in the background is from a production batch earlier than 359 – it is fitted with engines with exhaust manifolds.

In November the squadron had five Pe-2 and one UPe-2 aircraft in its inventory. Soon a second dual control trainer was delivered (s/n 20-418). This aircraft had been operated by 3. PLB from April 1945 till the disbandment of the regiment. The technical conditions of the Pe-2 aircraft of the Long Range Reconnaissance Squadron, some of the crews of which flew solely this type, was deteriorating. Three Pe-2s were unserviceable due to failures of VK-105PF engines. Despite constant efforts by the maintenance crews to keep these aircraft flying, failures of weary engines occurred. When the pilots were trying to increase RPM, the engines reacted with "power stall". Weary armament often failed. The electric wiring burnt, unable to withstand the overcharging, hence increasingly more "high-ampere" circuit breakers were used. The Pe-2 aircraft flew for the last time in parade formation over Gdynia on the Navy Day on 28 June 1953. The service of these weary aircraft in the Naval Aviation was coming to an end. Despite the efforts and sacrifice of the ground crews to keep these aircraft in airworthy condition, failures persisted.

In 1953 a Pe-2 made an emergency belly landing on grass at Babie Doły air base due to engine failure. 1st Lt Zdzisław Olszewski (pilot) and 1st Lt Lucjan Marcinkiewicz (naviga-

tor) escaped unhurt and the damaged aircraft was scrapped. Rhythmic rumble of Pe-2 and Tu-2 piston engines was soon silenced in Polish skies, giving way to the roar of jet engines. During the air parade over Gdynia on 28 June 1953 Lim-1 jet fighters from 34th Naval Fighter Aviation Regiment (34. PLM MW) were displayed for the first time. Pe-2 aircraft were retired from the Naval Aviation in 1954 and scrapped.

To answer the question of what the Pe-2 was like and how did it fly it is worth listening to the opinions of airmen who flew them.

Col. Tadeusz Dalecki became acquainted with the Pe-2 during training in the USSR at flying school in Engels. He described it as follows: "*The Pe-2 was an outstanding dive bomber, but had the disadvantage that it was difficult to keep flying on one engine and when both failed it fell down like an stone. However, there was someone who masterfully got himself out of this situation, when on return from a training flight both engines cut off and the propellers stopped. According to instructions, the crew should immediately have bailed out. The commander of the training regiment, Maj. Pyerov, risked landing the falling bomber. Although the bomber was falling down like a stone, he did not lose control. He dived to gain speed and made a swift approach to land. He landed*

42

at the airfield without crashing, within the landing marks. He saved the precious aircraft. It was a famed event, not only at our school, but in the entire bomber force. Pyerov was distinguished with a special citation and received a valuable prize".

According to Col. Kazimierz Wierzbicki, who commenced training on Pe-2 in 1944 in the USSR at Uzmorye air base *"it was one of the prettiest aircraft, but – as it turned out later – also the most difficult to fly. The opinion around the school was not good and caused our apprehension. Learning the landing technique in this aircraft was not easy. Early in the training all pilot made quite hard landings after which the inspection of landing gear and engine mounts showed no damage, but marks on the landing gear struts revealed that the shock absorbers were compressed to the maximum"*. Kazimierz Wierzbicki continued flying the Pe-2 as a first lieutenant in 7. SPLBN, where he was appointed commander of the 1st Squadron. He continued flying these bombers as a captain and from 1952 the commander of 35. PLB. Here are his remarks about flying the Pe-2: *"The Pe-2 aircraft, on which we had been training for three years, were specially adapted for diving. Their ruggedness and special devices allowed diving at 50, 70 or even 80-degree angles. At higher dive angles bombing accuracy was better. After having reached the pre-briefed altitude the navigator helped the pilot to commence the bombing run. The pilot, maintaining altitude, speed and heading waited for the navigator's signal to deploy the dive brakes. It reduced the airspeed by about 40 km/h and caused the aircraft's nose to drop. The pilot had to maintain previous speed increasing engine RPM and balance using the elevator trim. Simultaneously with the dive brakes the automatic bomb release and dive recovery mechanism was activated. After several seconds the navigator would pat the pilot on the shoulder and say "enter". It was a very important moment. The pilot pushed on the control column with a smooth, but vigorous move, watching the aircraft's behaviour. The pilot should enter the dive at higher angle than briefed previously, simultaneously trying to lock on the target, keeping it in the crosshairs of the bomb sight mounted in front of his face. About 100 meters before the bomb release altitude the navigator gave signal to recover in the same way as previously. The pilot pushed the button on the right handle of the control yoke and the automatic mechanism released the bombs and recovered the aircraft from the dive. Despite the use of dive brakes the airspeed built up very quickly, up to 600–700 km/h at recovery, which means that it increased by 300–400 km/h in comparison with the dive entry speed in several seconds. The loss of altitude amounted to 800–1500 m, depending on the entry speed and dive angle. The g-loads during the recovery were high, causing temporary blackout and loss of consciousness. The gunner/wireless operators, seated in the aft section, were in worse situation. There is no wonder that they were not enthusiastic about these missions. Sometimes the dive recovery mechanism failed. In such situation the pilot had to pull the control column with all his might, sometimes with navigator's assistance"*.

[43-44]: Preflight check of Pe-2 cockpit hatch locking mechanism in the 7. PLB, Malbork 1951.

[45]: *A Pe-2 with white number "5" on the inboard surface of the tail fin.*

[46]: *Inboard side of VK-105PF engine nacelle with the exhaust manifold.*

Diving in a three-ship formation was even more sophisticated and demanded excellent formation flying skills and ability to react quickly in most difficult situations.

Lt Col. Janusz Łukaszewicz, who dreamed about being a fighter pilot, was assigned to bomber pilot training group at Dęblin flying school. Here is his opinion about the Pe-2: *"It was obvious that flying the Pe-2 would not be a pleasure. It was an aircraft difficult to fly and to maintain... These aircraft were the main equipment of the Soviet Air Force bomber units during the Second World War and were quite aged and their wartime service left its stamp on them. First the entire Bomber Pilot Class 20, consisting of ten pilots, completed training on the UTB-2, having made about 40 sorties with an instructor in about six hours, amassing an average of 15 flight hours per pilot. Unfortunately, the school did not receive Tu-2 aircraft, so we had to fly the Peshka. Even during preparations for flying it turned out that it would not be easy. The Pe-2 was known for not tolerating serious flying errors. On take-off it had a tendency to veer off from the right direction. During flight the pilot had to maintain prescribed speeds precisely and "bouncing" on landing was a normal thing, making every beginner pilot astounded.*

[47-48}: Cockpit canopy typical for Pe-2 aircraft from 205th production batch onwards, with the mast of RSBF-5 radio wire antenna mounted atop the windshield frame. The air data probes and outside air thermometer are mounted on top of the mast.

What was worse, off the first small bounce it could make another one, even bigger. Some of our instructors, those with more wild imagination claimed that with the fourth bounce the Peshka can jump over the hangar. Even after a successful touchdown, on the landing run the pilot still had to be alert, because a dangerous situation still might occur. I have to admit that the Peshka educated us deeply. We made our first solo flights after having flown about 10 hours with an instructor on the UPe-2 dual control trainer version, called Shparka. The first solo flight on the combat version was made without the rest of the crew and without retracting the landing gear, which made flying more complicated".

Col. Aleksander Milart was an instructor pilot, squadron commander in the Dęblin flying school, training Pe-2 pilots and later was the commander of the 21st Reconnaissance Aviation Regiment and 55th Transport Aviation Regiment. Here is his account of the Pe-2: "The Pe-2 had two features. It had a beautiful silhouette in the air and was very difficult to fly and perform combat missions. Only the best and physically strongest cadet pilots were selected for training on it. The school commander was

ordered to send a Pe-2 to the Polish Army Museum in Warsaw. I was tasked with preparing one aircraft to be an exhibit. I decided to get rid of one of the airplanes which the Russians did not want to fly. I continued this tradition as the commander. They said it was very difficult to land. It never guaranteed safe landing. On this particular airplane it was dangerous. A three-point landing was almost impossible. When the main wheels touched the ground, pulling on the control column caused bouncing. When one tried to correct the bouncing, every next bounce was higher, and after speed loss the aircraft tipped on the wing, which could be easily broken. This airplane was incorrectly set up in the factory and that was the result. Allowing the cadet pilots to fly it was out of the question. I made a check flight and, knowing its quirks, wrote

[49]: *Gunner/wireless operator Kazimierz Jamrozik in open compartment with the canopy raised. A small, semi-circular glazing around the 7.62 mm ShKAS machine gun port is visible. A 12.7 mm UBT machine gun is installed in navigator's rotating turret. The camouflage is faded.*

[50]: *A pilot in the sliding-back canopy upper window. The aerodynamic compensator (so-called "ear") is visible atop the VUB-1 gun turret. The Pe-2 "20" in faded paint scheme is visible in the background.*

a protocol of unairworthiness. It was low on total flying time, but the engineers prepared proper documentation and the goal was achieved. The aircraft was dismantled, but the fuselage with wing centre section remained as one piece. The aircraft, towed by a truck and tractor, arrived in Warsaw after a three-day journey, on 10 August 1950. The roads were narrow those days, with thick trees on both sides, which had to be zig-zagged by. At the museum the airplane was reassembled and put on display next to others. When I was visiting the museum after many years, I saw my Peshka. I felt like a father of this exhibit. I was sorry. The airplane was neglected. The cockpit glazing was broken, the paint was dirty and flaking. I tried to get the airplane transferred to the Polish Aviation Museum in Cracow, but it proved impossible due to various dependences of both museums. It is a pity, because in Cracow the aircraft would have been better cared for Aleksander Milart, Kraków, 11 August 2011". The Pe-2 remained at the Polish Army Museum and was later restored.

Captain Kazimierz Gawron included an opinion about these aircraft in his memoirs, with hindsight of many years after their retirement. He was a navigator on Pe-2 and made 188 flights, totalling 109 hours and 38 min. He described also the handling qualities of this bomber aircraft, operated in largest number by post-war Polish military aviation. According to him the Pe-2 was too difficult to fly for nervous pilots with flying skills below average. A Pe-2 crew of the Long Range Reconnaissance Squadron of 30. PL MW learned it the hard way when the unit was based at Słupsk. Ens. Kazimierz Gawron was the navigator and Edward Kuper was the gunner/wireless operator. The aircraft commander, 2nd Lt "X", made the round out too high before every landing and the aircraft plopped down on the runway in various, always odd, positions. It was then said in Russian *na tri tochki po odinochki* – on each wheel separately, instead of on three points, to comply with aircraft's operating manual. The aircraft bounced like a ball, sometimes reared on the tailwheel. Since there was no habit of fastening safety belts, the navigator had to grab the machine gun mount to avoid head injury during these "stunts". However, it was not the last flight, during which pilot "X", unable to cope with flying the Pe-2, caused a dangerous situation. During a cross-country navigation flight in fine weather he almost caused the aircraft to stall and spin. The navigator recalled it: *"Being busy with the map and my log initially I didn't notice the abnormal situation, that the aircraft was flying with the nose offset at high angle to the course, one wing deep below the horizon and the other one pointing to the sky. The upset pilot made an immediate return to base. In order to not increase the already deep bank the aircraft made a big "regional" turn and landed safely, but hard. The situation was explained on the ground by the squadron commander. It turned out that the pilot had set the trim tab in the wrong direction. Instead of balancing the aileron, making flying the aircraft easier, he did it in reverse."*

The situation of navigator and gunner/wireless operator changed radically in April 1950, when pilot "X" left the unit and 1st Lt Edward Mataczun, a truly outstanding pilot, became the aircraft commander. In his hands the Pe-2 flew like a fighter aircraft. He wanted to become a fighter pilot, but at the beginning of the training he was assigned to dive bombers. When he was flying, there were no "regional" turns and dangerous landings. Here are further interesting and well balanced remarks of Capt. Gawron about this dive bomber. *"Despite numerous technical shortcomings the Pe-2 was good in the hands of a skilled pilot. In this respect it was a "hot" aircraft, obviously within the limitations*

[51]: *A Pe-2 with camouflage splotches visible on the wings, photographed at Piła airfield.*

[52]: A Pe-2 tied down on a grass airfield. A "tray", protecting the tyre against the noxious effect of coolant and gas leaks, is visible above the tarpaulin-covered wheel. Standing next to the propeller is 1st Lt Skomorowski.

[53]: A commemorative photo with a Pe-2. The line between the blue and olive green is visible on the side of the engine nacelle.

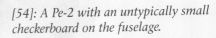

[54]: A Pe-2 with an untypically small checkerboard on the fuselage.

of a bomber aircraft. Lt Mataczun repeatedly said that he could make a barrel roll – a figure typical for a fighter aircraft. I suppose the aircraft would withstand it. I had no doubts about the skills of my aircraft commander, but fortunately he did not conduct this experiment. However, the aircraft was not safe. Its twin engines required very coordinated flight control operations and violations of this rule caused crashes, in which usually the entire crews were killed, also on approach to landing. Compact and robust construction allowed errors on touchdown; the landing gear was so elastic that after an erroneous approach the aircraft bounced on touchdown better than a well – inflated ball. Some pilots, those who were not adept at this quite difficult manoeuver, owed the integrity of their bones and those of their subordinates, locked in cockpit during these "stunts", to the landing gear of Pe-2. And there was something to behold, when every bounce against the concrete runway pitched the aircraft in a different, often even more troublesome attitude, so the eventual result was often hard to predict. If I say that I know cases of going around – i.e. an emergency take-off from that position – one may imagine the height of the bounce. The risk that one of the engine, abruptly set to take-off power would not "unwind" froze the spectators by the knowledge that they might witness another crash, let alone the feelings of the crew. The malicious claimed that a special thanks for the landing gear design was the epitaph on the designer's tomb."

One of the navigator's duties was operating the electrically driven hydraulic pump for landing gear lowering and retracting. With the poor condition of the electric system of the weary Pe-2 aircraft the circuit breakers often burned. It necessitated replacement of the circuit breakers in the central distribution box, called "tseersha" from Russian, in flight. When it did not help, the navigator had to lower the landing gear manually.

The bomb release and aiming equipment of the Pe-2 was not sophisticated. The navigator usually released the bombs electrically. The OPB-1r (*opticheski pritsel bombardirovshchika*) telescopic bombsight was fitted with an electric bomb release switch, connected with the bomb racks via the bomb release mechanism. The emergency mechanical bomb release lever, which opened the bomb bay doors, was mounted on the port side of the navigator's compartment. It enabled jettisoning the bomb load in emergency situations (such as in-flight fire, necessity of emergency landing or electric system failure). Operating it before passing the IP (Initial Point of the bombing run) and before the arrival over the bombing range was prohibited. Pressing the knob on the bomb

[55-56]: *Groundcrews working on the VK-105PF engines of a Pe-2 aircraft in the 7. PLB.*

[57]: *Posing in front of a Pe-2 of the 30. PL MW is its crew: Lt Hilary Zarucki (pilot), Ens. Tadeusz Pawlaczek (navigator), and gunner/wireless operator, Chief Petty Officer Jerzy Raj, Babie Doły 1952.*

[58]: *Gunner/wireless operator Petty Officer Kazimierz Jamrozik posing in his open compartment in a Pe-2 of 30. PL MW (30th Air Regiment of Navy Aviation).*

release mechanism lever opened the bomb bay doors. On the lever also a small handle, called the "spoon", was mounted, pressing of which jettisoned the bomb load. To avoid releasing bombs while opening the bomb bay doors the navigator had to obey the rule "do not hold the spoon when opening the bomb bay doors". Despite this Pe-2 navigators made several such errors and the bombs were dropped in the wrong place.

Pe-2 pilots dropped the bombs only in a dive. The bombs were then carried on external racks under the wing centre section. After 1949, due to the wear of Pe-2 aircraft, dive bombing was abandoned. Recovery from the dive in a Pe-2 was not a safe manoeuver. The heavy, twin-engine airplane rapidly losing altitude could be recovered to horizontal attitude only by the pilot's strength. For this purpose the *Peshka* was fitted with dive brakes, limiting the very high diving speed, and automatic dive recovery mechanism, changing the tailplane's angle of incidence, facilitating the recovery. However, there were cases that the automatic recovery mechanism failed in a decisive moment and the pilot, aided by the navigator, recovered the aircraft with ultimate effort, just above the ground. Some did not manage to do it... When dive bombing was abandoned, the redundant dive brakes were removed to reduce drag, as well as the automatic dive recovery mechanisms. The Pe-2 was not equipped for long flights without ground visibility. The Pe-2s were not flown without external visual reference to ground and in instrument flying meteorological conditions. The pilots made only training flights in covered cockpits ("under the hood") in the air manoeuvering zone and cross-country. Nobody dared to fly into thick clouds or above clouds in the Pe-2. The aircraft was not fitted with ice protection systems and icing in the clouds caused a crash hazard. In January 1952 a well-trained crew could fly a Pe-2 in daylight, with horizontal visibility 4 km and cloud base 200 m. It shows the technical quality of aircraft and airfield equipment in those days.

Pe-2 flights to altitudes of 4,500 and 5,000 m and bombing from these altitudes were classified as high-altitude missions. For these missions the crews donned fur-lined flight suits, boots, gloves and flying helmets. For climbing to the altitude of 4,500 m the crew members were given an egg and bar of chocolate immediately after landing by the catering officer, present at the flightline.

The range of the Pe-2 did not allow long flights. The longest flight on this type in the Long Range Reconnaissance Squadron, recorded in the log book of Lt JG K. Gawron, on the brink of the aircraft's range with necessary fuel reserve lasted 1 hour and 46 minutes. (On the Tu-2S – 3 hours 15 minutes). Neither the Pe-2, nor the Tu-2S, were intended for long range reconnaissance missions, contrary to what the Naval Aviation squadron's name might suggest. As a dive bomber the Pe-2 was intended for ground troop support, attacking fixed and mobile targets on enemy territory, but not far beyond the front line – the limited combat radius allowed only this. The Pe-2s flew over the Polish sea only with good visibility and high cloud base. Hence during flights in the coastal area, with the coastline characteristic of the Baltic Sea, the loss of orientation was rather unlikely.

[59]: *The Pe-2 aircraft in the 30. PL MW were marked with the outer surfaces of lower tail fin tips and the entire spinners (as shown), or their forward sections, painted white.*

[60]: *The Pe-2 aircraft in 30. PL MW were marked with white lower tips of the tail fins. The mechanic in the foreground is Petty Officer Wójtowicz.*

[61]: *A Pe-2 of the 21. PLZ prior to take-off for a training sortie from Sochaczew-Bielice airfield. The port engine is already running at high RPM and the starboard engine is just starting up.*

[62-63]: A Pe-2 adapted in 1950 by the Chief Aviation Institute for the role of a flying testbed for a supersonic ramjet engine, designed by Dr Eng. Stanisław Wójcicki. The mount with the tested engine was fitted atop the fuselage. However, testing of the supersonic engine on the too slow bomber was abandoned. In 1952 the mount and engine were removed and the aircraft was returned to the Air Force.

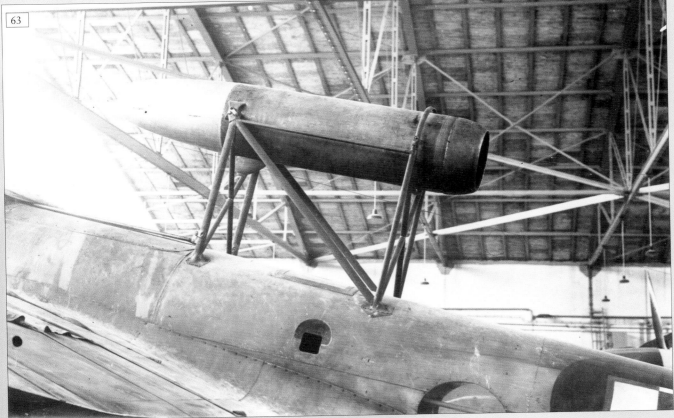

The main photographic equipment of the Pe-2 in the Naval Aviation were AFA-im cameras, intended for fighter aircraft. They allowed taking single or serial photographs, the remaining settings of these cameras could be adjusted only on ground.

The pilot took the seat in the cockpit first, followed by the navigator. Both entered the cockpit through the ventral hatch with pull-out step beneath the forward fuselage. Ground crew closed the hatch and the navigator locked it from inside. The gunner/wireless operator entered his compartment though a hatch beneath the middle fuselage section, which opened to the inside, and locked it. The Pe-2 cockpit was cramped "like a barrel". The lack of room in the cockpit was bothersome, particularly for the navigator when he was manning the 12.7 mm UBT machine gun, installed behind his back in a rotating turret. The rods of the machine gun mount and expended cartridge case caught permanently on the parachute harness and hampered moving around the extremely cramped cockpit (the comparison between the cockpits of Pe-2 and Tu-2S, operated later, was like between the Syrena and Fiat 125p cars). To fire the gun the navigator had to fold his uncomfortable round seat, suspended on metal supports over the always unreliable and dangerous hatch, and turn his back to the direction of flight. Sometimes the guns fired continuously until the ammunition was expended. The hatch was a separate matter. One could never be sure if it would not open at the most inappropriate moment. Therefore standing on it was prohibited in any circumstances, as it opened to the outside. There were cases of loss of the hatch in flight. It is easy to imagine the draft in the cockpit at a speed exceeding 300 km/h, let alone other possible results of this situation. "*It is puzzling that in preparing for the sorties we practised various, also emergency situations, we did not practice abandoning the aircraft in flight (obviously on the ground). There were questions what to do in case of fire, flight controls jamming, hung-up bombs and other problems we could encounter in the air, but the bail out situations were not discussed. There was a* conspiracy of silence *about bailing out from the Pe-2, or this problem was addressed very theoretically. It was not only the fear of "tempting the misfortune", as the aviators are rather not superstitious. The issue seems obvious: the formula for bailing out from these aircraft must have been indeterminate due to the design of the cockpit canopy, common for the pilot and navigator. It concerned the gunner/wireless operator to lesser extent, whose ventral hatch provided better chances for relatively safe bailout*".

Despite continuous efforts of the maintenance personnel, keeping the squadron's aircraft airworthy was increasingly more

[64]: *An early production Pe-2 in the Air Technical School in Zamość. In March 1945 this aircraft was delivered to the Military Flying School, from where it was passed to the ATS. It was identified as Pe-2R. Similar, extensive side nose glazing was characteristic for the Pe-2 bombers of 18ᵗʰ through 31ˢᵗ production batches. The airplane was used as a technical aid in engine and airframe technician training. Its M-105RA engines were serviceable wings starting them up was practised. Zamość, April 1945.*

[65]: *Cadet officers posing in front of the "weary" tail fin of the last Pe-2 in the Officer Aviation School in Dęblin. Standing left to right: Zygmunt Gruszczyk, Jerzy Legut and Mieczysław Dąbrowski. The photo was taken in 1956.*

[66]: *A Pe-2 standing at Zamość school. Two Yak-9s and probably an UT-2 aircraft are visible in the background. In front of the Yak-9M with three portraits behind it, a banner with propaganda slogan:* "Let's follow the example of the Stalin's Falcons – the heroes of the Soviet Union". *In front of the Pe-2 a plaque with instruction:* "Keep off the grass! Watching aircraft is permitted only from the pavements" *visible.*

difficult and time-consuming. The engines of Pe-2 aircraft from older production batches had lower power than the nominal output. The pilots, working the "throttle" intensely at high RPM to obtain proper power output of the weary engines, caused the cylinder heads and engine blocks to overheat, which resulted in a "power stall". The coolant penetrated through burnt-out seals to the cylinders. It caused significant drop in power, "coughing" and dangerous consequences. It was upsetting, particularly when flying over the sea. The navigators had to observe carefully if water or steam was leaking from under the cowlings or exhaust pipes… The technical condition of weary Pe-2 aircraft operated by the Long Range Reconnaissance Squadron was deteriorating and failures occurred increasingly more often, eventually leading to a serious engine failure and emergency landing at Babie Doły air base on 14 August 1953.

"Our Pe-2s were increasingly less safe in the air. I like flying this aircraft, it was undoubtedly attractive. The afterthought that it was not a safe aircraft came much later – in fact when it was a museum exhibit. Maybe it is better…"

Paint schemes and markings of Pe-2 aircraft

The Pe-2 aircraft from the 1st Bombardment Division, formed in the latter half of 1944 in the USSR, wore – as can be seen in photographs from that time – multi-coloured camouflage, applied in compliance with two possible schemes contained in a wartime instruction[1]. The surfaces visible from above and sides had camouflage consisting of dark green, tan and dark

grey splotches. The surfaces visible from below were light blue. Transitions between the colours were blurred. Distinct, sharp boundaries between the colours are visible only in a few photographs. The aircraft wore red stars, the national insignia of the USSR, on lower wing surfaces, fuselage sides and vertical tail surfaces. Large white and red checkerboards were painted on both sides of the nose, in front of the cockpit. On 4 April 1945 the command of 1st Bombardment Division ordered introduction of a unified system of identification of aircraft assignment to respective regiments, squadrons within the regiments, as well as markings of the aircraft of the regiment commanders and their deputies. Assignment of aircraft to respective regiments was denoted by the colour of the forward sections of the spinners and lower section of the vertical tail surfaces. In 3. PLB it was red, in 4. PLB blue and in 5. PLB yellow. The assignment of aircraft to respective squadrons within the regiment was denoted by the colour of the squadron numbers, 50 cm in height. In the regiments' first squadrons the numbers were black, in the second squadrons white and in the third squadrons yellow. The digits of the numbers had red outlines. The squadron numbers were painted on the inner sides of the vertical tail surfaces. Airplanes of the regiment commanders were marked with three rings on the noses and three stripes on the lower sections of the vertical tail surfaces in colours assigned to the respective regiments. However, photographs of airplanes of the regiment commanders with three rings on the noses are not yet known. However, photos of airplanes of the regiment commanders show other markings on the noses – arrows with small heads and narrow rays in lieu of the rings.

In the 7. SPLBN the arrow on commander's airplane had the shape of lightning. The airplanes assigned to deputy regiment commanders were distinguished by arrows with large heads and expanding rays, painted on both sides of the nose,

---

1   The directive n°2389/0133 of 3 July, 1943, gave new instructions to paint the Soviet warplanes. The directive assumed that the non-fighter planes had to be delivered with the new camouflage starting from 1 August 1943. The directive contained 15 camouflage schemes for many types, of which 2 were for Pe-2.

and three vertical stripes on the lower section of vertical tail surfaces, denoting the assignment to individual regiments.

Among Pe-2 aircraft from later deliveries, arriving from the end of the war till September 1945, were examples from Soviet Air Force materiel reserves. Among them were airplanes in an overall grey paint scheme. During the overhauls of Pe-2 and UPe-2 aircraft, beginning in late 1947, upper and side surfaces were painted olive green and the surfaces visible from below were still painted light blue. In the Dęblin school Pe-2 aircraft wearing multi-coloured camouflage were still operated as late as 1949, as the photos taken then show.

In July 1945 re-painting of national insignia began. The red stars were painted over (sometimes not very carefully) and replaced by white and red checkerboards, 100 cm in width on lower wing surfaces, 70 cm on fuselage sides and 50 cm on the vertical tail surfaces. The checkerboards on the noses were often left not painted over for some time. Cases of applying checkerboards with reversed colour scheme were quite frequent. Later, after the disbandment of two regiments and forming of 7. SPLBN, painting aircraft tail numbers in different colours to denote their assignment to respective squadrons was abandoned. The tail numbers were painted on the inner sides of the vertical tail surfaces or on the fuselage. On Pe-2 aircraft operated by 30. PL MW the forward spinner sections and lower sections of outer sides of the vertical tail surfaces were painted white.

[67]: The commander of 35. PLB, Maj. K. Wierzbicki (second from left) at Przasnysz airfield, when the 35th Regiment ended operations of Pe-2 bombers and left these aircraft there to be scrapped.

[68]: A Pe-2 and a hangar with an erased slogan about Stalin's Falcons in the background.

[69]: A Pe-2 with the marking of deputy regiment commander in the form of an arrow, probably red with white outline. The spinners are probably red.

[70]: Pe-2 bombers standing at the flightline. The airplane second from left is the deputy regiment commander's airplane, marked with an arrow. The spinners are two-colour, probably white and red.

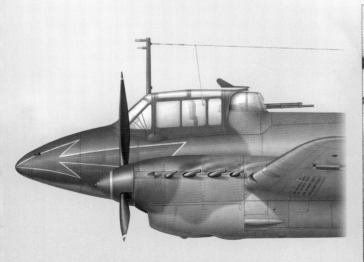

[71]: A three-colour spinner on a Pe-2 marked with an arrow typical for a deputy regiment commander. The photo was taken in the 7ᵗʰ Regiment at Ławica airfield.

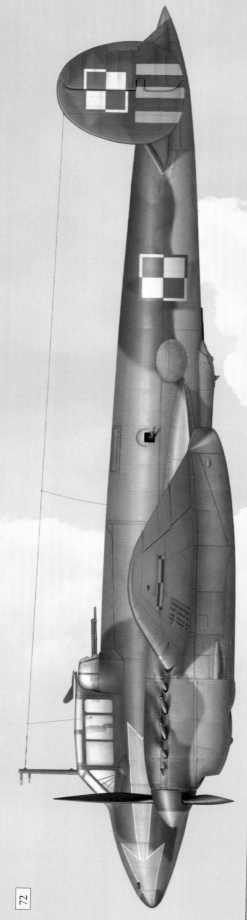

[72]: Petlyakov Pe-2 of the deputy commander of the 5. PLB, Sochaczew 1945. Aircraft in wartime paint scheme consisting of dark green (AMT-4), light brown (AMT-21) and dark grey (AMT-12) splotches on upper surfaces and light blue (AMT-7) under surfaces. Yellow arrow with white outline, yellow spinner tips, three vertical yellow stripes on the tail fins. Red rudder trim tab.

[74]: The airplane wearing markings of deputy regimental commander and reversed checkerboards is visible in the foreground, among four aircraft taking off from the airfield of Sochaczew.

[73]: The Pe-2 of the deputy commander of the 5. PLB, marked with a yellow arrow with white outline and broadening head. Soviet groundcrews pose in front of the aircraft, with only one soldier wearing a Polish four-cornered cap visible amount them – a personnel situation typical for that period. Sochaczew, July 1945.

[75]: *Petlyakov Pe-2 with markings of the deputy commander of the 7. SPLBN, Modlin, September 1946. Aircraft in wartime paint scheme. Red arrow with white outline, red spinner tips, three vertical red stripes on the tail fins and rudder trim tab. The checkerboards have very thin outlines.*

[77]: *A doctored photo of the Pe-2 of the deputy commander of the 7. SPLBN, marked with a red arrow with white outline on the nose and three vertical red stripes on the tail fin. The checkerboards have very thin outlines. The photograph was taken probably before the air parade over Bydgoszcz on 1 September 1946.*

[76]: *Refuelling of a Pe-2 from a ZiS-5V bowser. The arrow and spinner tips are of similar colour.*

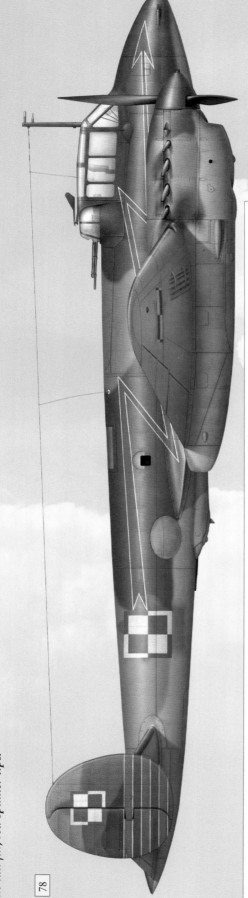

[78]: Petlyakov Pe-2 of the commander of the 7. SPLBN, Ławica, 1948. Aircraft in wartime paint scheme. Twice folded lightning and three red stripes with white outlines on the tail fin, red spinner tips.

[79]: A 1948 photo of the Pe-2 of the commander of the 7. SPLBN, with a small checkerboard on the tail fin and lightning with the rear end just next to the checkerboard edge. The airman second from right is Adam Wierzykowski, the crew chief of Col. Bortnikov's aircraft and later the engineer of the 30. PL MW.

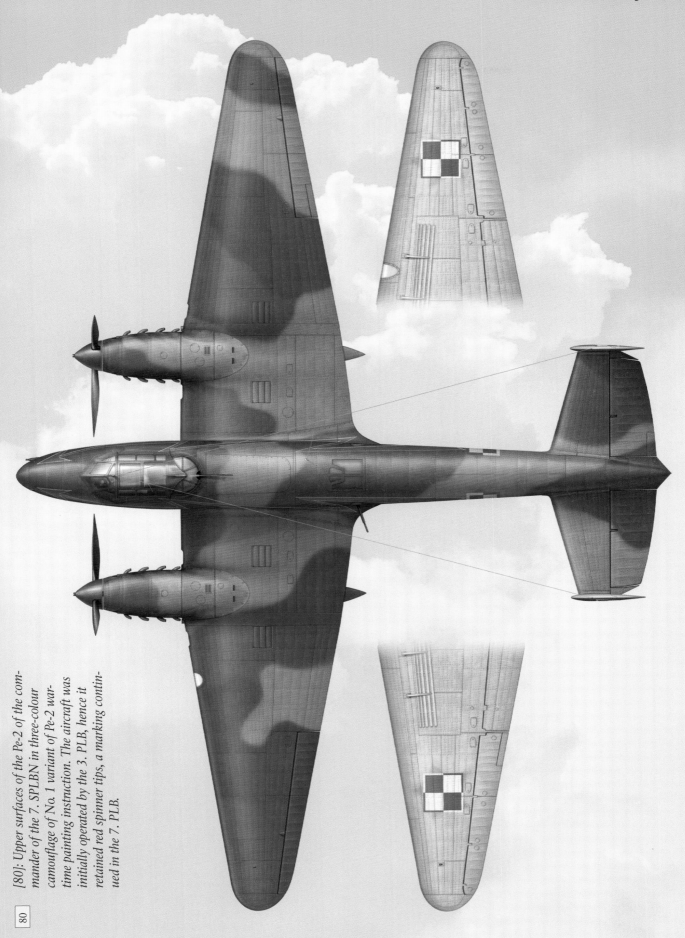

[80]: Upper surfaces of the Pe-2 of the commander of the 7. SPLBN in three-colour camouflage of No. 1 variant of Pe-2 wartime painting instruction. The aircraft was initially operated by the 3. PLB, hence it retained red spinner tips, a marking continued in the 7. PLB.

80

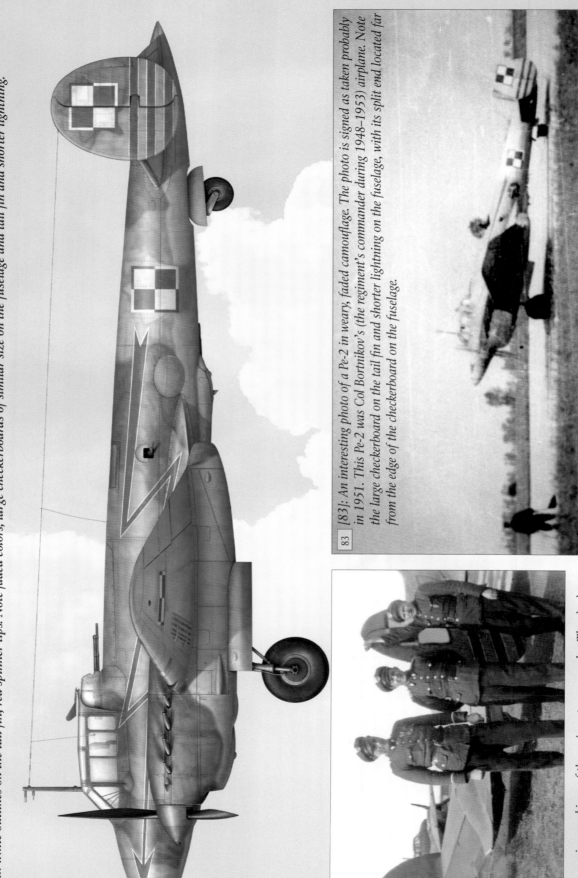

[81]: Pettyakov Pe-2 of Col. Mikhail Bortnikov, the commander of 7. PBN (Dive Bomber Regiment) in 1951. The wartime paint scheme. Twice folded lightning and three red stripes with white outlines on the tail fin, red spinner tips. Note faded colors, large checkerboards of similar size on the fuselage and tail fin and shorter lightning.

81

[83]: An interesting photo of a Pe-2 in weary, faded camouflage. The photo is signed as taken probably in 1951. This Pe-2 was Col Bortnikov's (the regiment's commander during 1948–1953) airplane. Note the large checkerboard on the tail fin and shorter lightning on the fuselage, with its split end located far from the edge of the checkerboard on the fuselage.

83

[82]: Pe-2 wearing markings of the regiment commander. The checkerboard on the tail fin is large, with thin outlines. Interesting is the fragment of the Pe-2 visible in the background, with early type of canopy and antenna mast fitted to the aft canopy frame.

82

[84]: Pe-2 yellow "8" with red outline from 7. SPLBN, May 1946. The wartime paint scheme. The airplane, taken over from the 3rd Squadron of the 3. PLB, has red lower part of the tail fin's outboard surface and spinner tip, white and red rudder trim tab and yellow number with red outline.

[85]: Pe-2 aircraft with numbers "8", "2" and "7". These aircraft, taken over from the 3. PLB, retained red lower tail fin sections. In the front row are nine aircraft of the parade formation and the leading Pe-2. Okęcie, 9 May 1946.

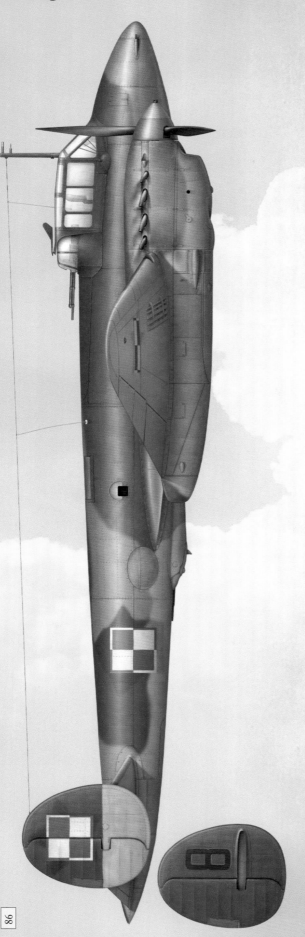

[86]: Pe-2 of the 3. PLB black "8", Leźnica Wielka 1946. The wartime paint scheme. The aircraft initially was assigned to the 1st Squadron, therefore it wears a black number with red outline. Yellow lower part of the tail fin reveals its previous assignment to the 4. PLB, where the spinner tips were also painted yellow, reversed checkerboard. Red rudder trim tab.

[87]: Eleven Pe-2s aircraft at Leźnica Wielka airfield in 1946. Four airplanes visible on the left wear reversed checkerboards. The second aircraft from left wears the number "9" on the inner side of the tail fin and the third from left has number "8".

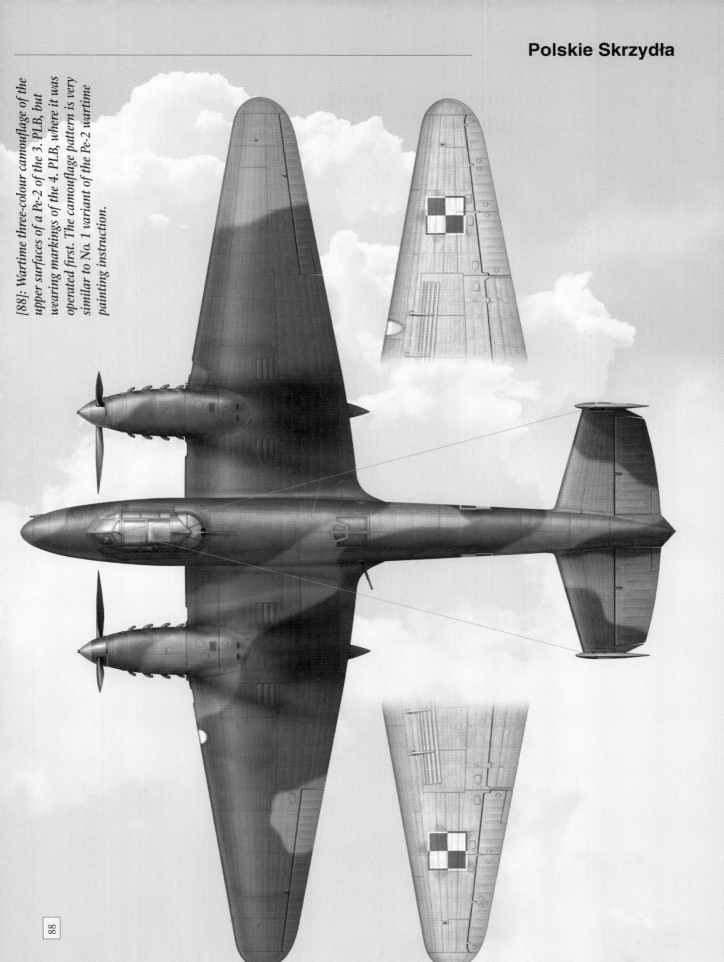

[88]: Wartime three-colour camouflage of the upper surfaces of a Pe-2 of the 3. PLB, but wearing markings of the 4. PLB, where it was operated first. The camouflage pattern is very similar to No 1 variant of the Pe-2 wartime painting instruction.

88

[89]: *Petlyakov Pe-2 yellow "8", Okęcie, September 1947. The wartime paint scheme. This airplane was initially assigned to the 4. PLB, disbanded in 1946, in which the lower section of tail fin outboard surfaces and spinner tips were painted light blue. On some aircraft the propeller blade tips were painted blue and separated from the remainder of the black propeller blade with a thin white stripe (as in the photo 10, page 8). Number with red outline and white/red rudder trim tab.*

[90]: *Three Pe-2 aircraft with numbers "8", "7" and "8", in wartime three-colour camouflage, before the display on 7 September 1947 in Warsaw. The number 8 on the third last airplane in the row has different shape than one two other airplanes standing at its left.*

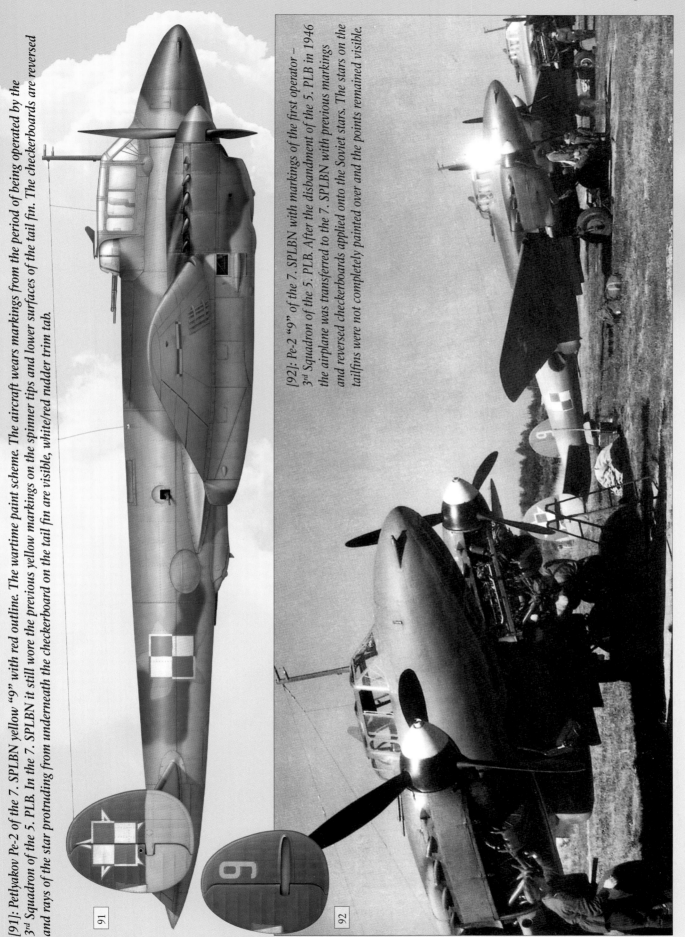

[91]: Petlyakov Pe-2 of the 7. SPLBN yellow "9" with red outline. The wartime paint scheme. The aircraft wears markings from the period of being operated by the 3rd Squadron of the 5. PLB. In the 7. SPLBN it still wore the previous yellow markings on the spinner tips and lower surfaces of the tail fin. The checkerboards are reversed and rays of the star protruding from underneath the checkerboard on the tail fin are visible, white/red rudder trim tab.

[92]: Pe-2 "9" of the 7. SPLBN with markings of the first operator – 3rd Squadron of the 5. PLB. After the disbandment of the 5. PLB in 1946 the airplane was transferred to the 7. SPLBN with previous markings and reversed checkerboards applied onto the Soviet stars. The stars on the tailfins were not completely painted over and the points remained visible.

[93]: Petlyakov Pe-2 with markings of the 5. PLB. The wartime paint scheme, the spinner tips and lower surfaces of the tail fin yellow. Yellow number 5 and white 11. It is not known which one of the two numbers visible on the tail fin was painted first. Red rudder trim tab.

[94]: A Pe-2 with running engines and flaps deployed to the take-off position. The airplane has double numbers: yellow "5" and white "11" on the inner side of the tail fin and reversed checkerboards. Lower tail fin sections and spinner tips are yellow.

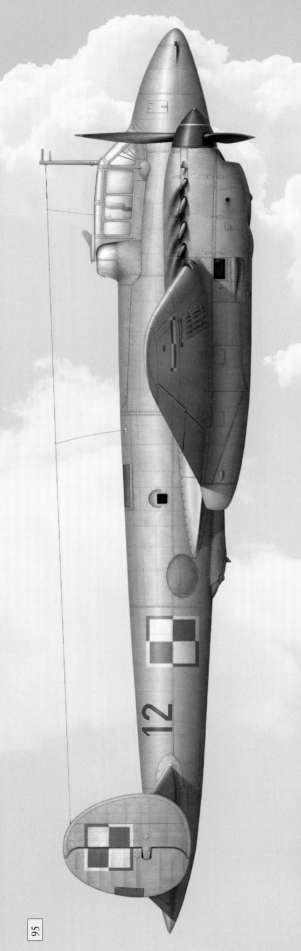

[95]: Pe-2 of the 7. SPLBN, red "12", delivered to Poland after the end of the war. Grey overall paint scheme. The number "12" was probably red and the spinner was of the same colour with a white stripe in the middle. There is no information how long this aircraft operated in this untypical paint scheme. Red rudder trim tab.

[97]: A Pe-2 in similar gray paint scheme to "12". Probably this is the same airplane.

[96]: One of several Pe-2 aircraft delivered to Poland between May and September 1945 in overall grey paint scheme. Open bomb bay in the aft section of the engine nacelle is visible. The number "12" and spinner are probably dark red. The forward and aft section of the spinner are separated with a white stripe.

[98]: Petlyakov Pe-2 of the 7. SPLBe, yellow "9". This airplane was standing together with three other Pe-2s (in wartime camouflage) for the bombing display at Okęcie airfield on the Aviation Day on 7 September 1947. Grey overall paint scheme, yellow number 9 with red outline on the inboard side of the tail fin. Large checkerboards are reversed and have thin outlines. The rudder trim tab is white and red.

98

[99]: Grey color of the upper surfaces of the Pe-2 "yellow 9" are visible. Dark streaks on the wings are made by gases from the exhaust pipes.

99

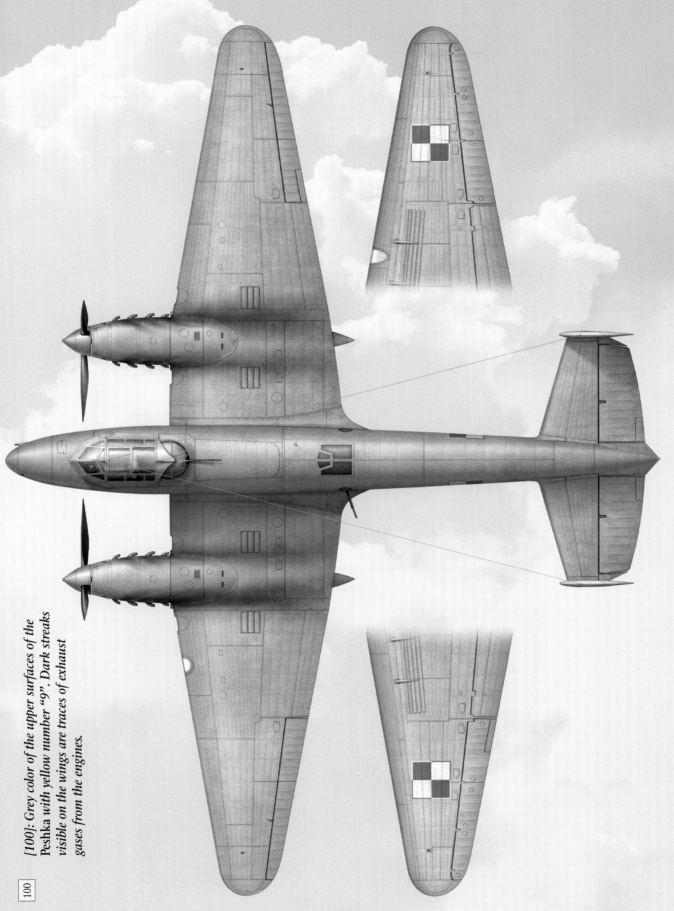

100

[100]: *Grey color of the upper surfaces of the Peshka with yellow number "9". Dark streaks visible on the wings are traces of exhaust gases from the engines.*

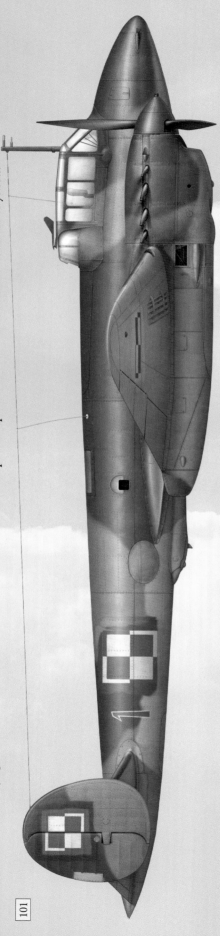

[101]: Petlyakov Pe-2, serial number 14-352, of the 3ʳᵈ Composite Training Squadron (3. Mieszana Eskadra Szkolna OSL w Dęblinie) of the Officer Flying School at Dęblin in 1946. The wartime camouflage scheme, with red number "1" with white outline. The spinner tips and are red and the rudder trim tab is yellow.

101

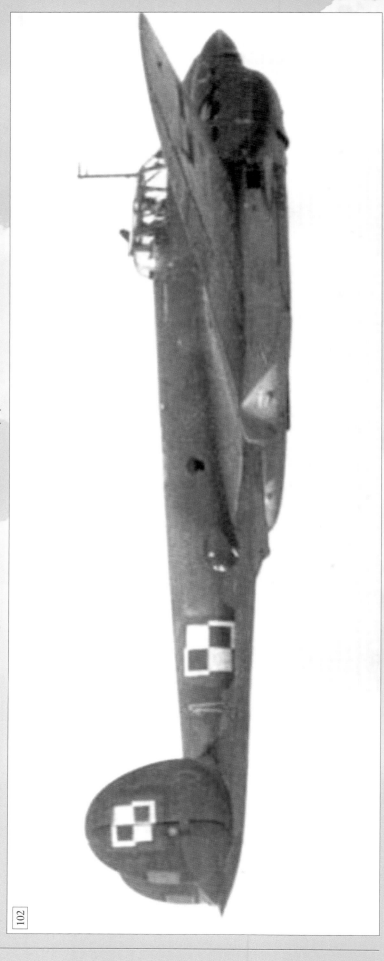

[102]: Pe-2 serial number 14-352 wearing wartime camouflage scheme, with red number "1" with white outline, operated by the 3ʳᵈ Composite Training Squadron of the Officer Flying School at Dęblin. This airplane was often flown by instructor pilot 1ˢᵗ Lt Aleksander Milart. Second half of 1946.

102

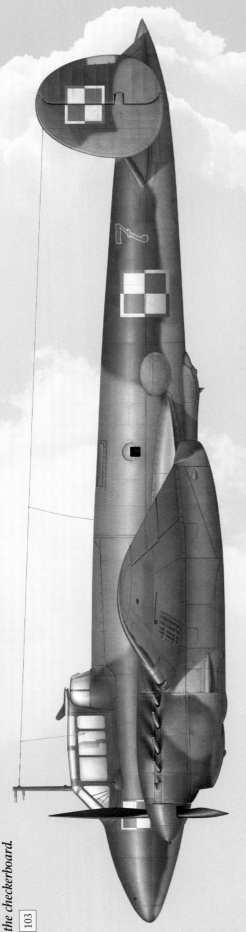

[103]: Pietlyakov Pe-2 red "7", operated by the Officer Flying School at Dęblin in 1946. The wartime camouflage scheme with three checkerboards on side surfaces, red stylized number "7" with white outline, red spinner and yellow rudder trim tab. The number "7" is visible near the trace of the painted-over star on the lower wing surface, without the checkerboard.

[104]

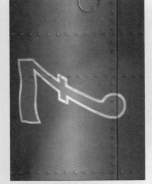

[104]: Pe-2 operated by the Officer Flying School in Dęblin in 1946, wearing wartime camouflage on upper and side surfaces. The aircraft has the red stars painted over, but the checkerboard on the nose remains. The spinners are red and the rudder trim tab is yellow. The checkerboards on the lower wing surfaces have not yet been applied.

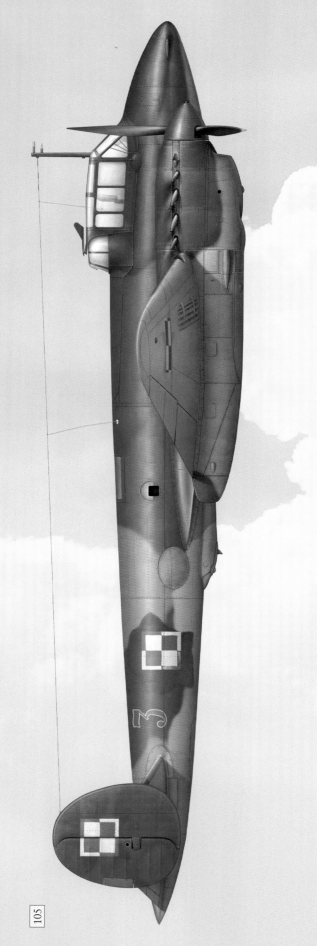

[105]: Petlyakov Pe-2 red "3", operated by the Officer Flying School in Dęblin. The wartime camouflage scheme. Red spinner and rudder trim tab, number 3 red with wihite outline.

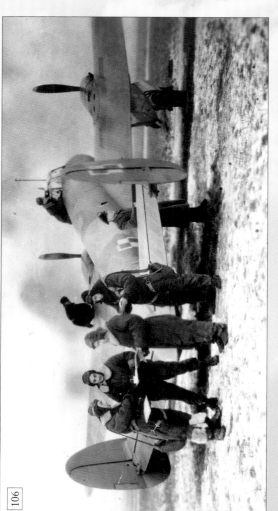

[106-107]: Two photographs of a Pe-2 in three-colour paint scheme, with stylized number "3", operated by Officer Flying School in Dęblin.

[108]: Petlyakov Pe-2 of the 7. PLB, white "15", Ławica 1950. Upper surfaces are olive green and lower surfaces are light blue. The spinner tip is red and there is no regiment marking on the tail fin.

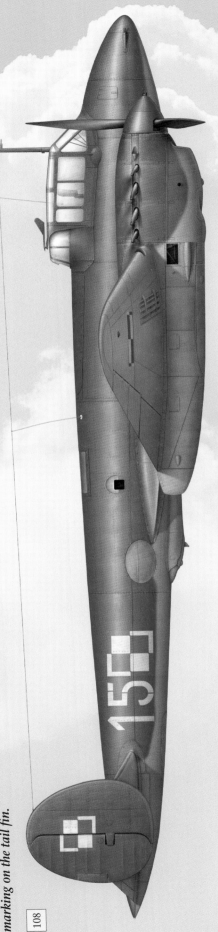

[108]

[109]

[109]: Technical inspection of 7. PLB aircraft. The Pe-2 "15", with olive green upper and side surfaces and light blue lower surfaces, is visible in the background. Behind it an UPe-2 with canvas-covered cockpits is visible. Ławica 1950.

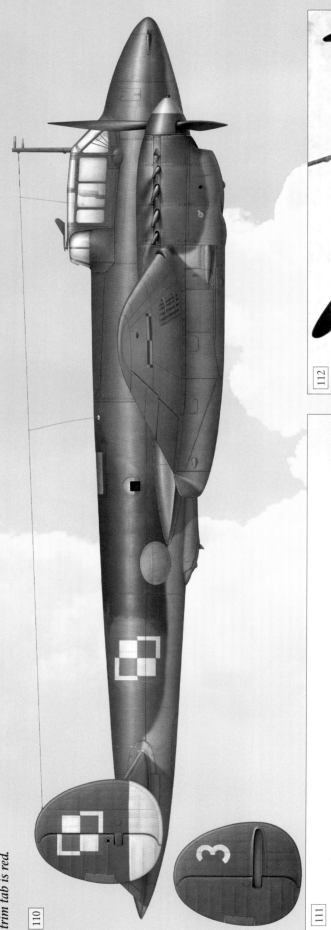

[110]: *Petlyakov Pe-2 white "3", serial number 13-357, of the 30. PL MW. Upper surfaces are olive green and lower surfaces are light blue, the darker part of the hull is the result of the renewal of the paint coating fragment. White outboard surfaces of the lower tail fin sections and white spinner tip, characteristic for this regiment. The rudder trim tab is red.*

[112]: *White spinner tip and lower tail fin section visible in this photo of the airplanes of the 30. PL MW.*

[111]: *The aft section of the Pe-2 "3", s/n 13-357, of the 30. PL MW with white outboard surfaces of the lower tail fin section. Dismantled cockpit canopy and gun turret dome lie under the airplane.*

[113]: Petlyakov Pe-2 white "15". Upper surfaces are olive green and lower surfaces are light blue. White horizontal stripe on the tail fin and spinner tip. Note clipped corners of the checkerboard.

[114]: A Pe-2 with white number "15" and horizontal stripe on the tail fin, adapted for aerial target towing.

Petlyakov UPe-2

From the beginning of Pe-2 bomber service it was noticed that their take-off and landing characteristics differed significantly from the widely used and easy to fly Tupolev SB aircraft. Therefore development of a dual control trainer version of the new dive bomber was necessary. The origins of the trainer ver-

sion of the Pe-2 bomber date back to February 1941. Then in Factory No. 22 two Pe-2 aircraft from the second production batch were fitted with dual controls in the navigator's compartment. One was handed over for evaluation to NII VVS (*Nauchno Isledovatelnyi Institut Voyenno – Vozdushnykh Sil*

[115-116]: UPe-2 aircraft of the Officer Flying School at Dęblin airfield in 1946. The large checkerboard on the nose is the remains of the wartime marking, denoting the aircraft's assignment to the 1st Bomber Aviation Division.

Krasnoy Armii – Red Army Air Force Scientific and Research Institute). The other one was assigned to 95th Combat Training Aviation Regiment. Parts of the dual controls, made of soft (in comparison with steel) duralumin were fragile, wore quickly and backlashes appeared in the axes and bushings of the dual control mechanism. Quickly wearing duralumin parts were replaced with steel ones. The instrument layout on the star-board instrument panel was changed and the navigator's seat was raised. These changes did little since the pilot's seat still obscured instructors' forward–left and forward–down vision. Flying the aircraft from instructor's position, it was impossible to land it on the runway. After repeated evaluation of the Pe-2 s/n 5-2 (fifth aircraft of the second production batch) with dual controls, conducted in May and June 1941 at NII VVS,

[116]: An UPe-2 with engines differing from each other in the exhaust systems. The starboard engine has exhaust manifolds, while the port one had individual exhaust stacks.

[118-119}: UPe-2 aircraft operated by the Officer Flying School in Dęblin, from production batches earlier than the 179th, therefore powered by engines with exhaust manifolds. The photo with a group of cadet officers was taken in 1947, after they completed navigator air training.

the opinion about this modification of the Pe-2 was negative. Such aircraft could not be used as a trainer.

After the German invasion on the USSR the main effort of the industry was focused on production of as many combat aircraft as possible. Bomber crew training continued in training units and combat regiments on the USB aircraft and the previous three-stage training was shortened. The elementary training was conducted on U-2 (Po-2) biplanes. During the second stage of training the pilot learned to fly the easy USB twin-engine aircraft. The transition to the Pe-2 was very difficult. Moreover, the flight time gained by pilots trained in reserve units was low. The level of skills of pilots arriving in the front-line units was insufficient. The situation could be improved only by development of fully capable trainer version of the Pe-2. During July and August 1942 Factory No. 22 produced further two trainer aircraft. The first of them, s/n 1-102, was sent for evaluation at NII VVS. It differed from the production Pe-2 bombers from the 102nd batch in having the instructor's cockpit in place of No. 1 fuel tank. The pilot and navigator's positions remained unaltered. The navigator's FT gun turret was removed and the space covered with a streamlined fairing made of plywood, called *gargrot* in Russian. Over the wing centre section was the instructor's cockpit with a windshield and aft-sliding canopy. The back of the instructor's cockpit was covered by a streamlined plywood fairing. Placing the instructor's cockpit above the wing centre section and trainee pilot and navigator's cockpit provided excellent visibility for the instructor. The instructor's cockpit was modestly equipped with instruments and controls in comparison with the trainee's cockpit. In some cases it had tragic consequences. Apart from the rudder, elevator and aileron controls the instructor's cockpit was equipped with flap, rudder and elevator trim switches. The wheel brakes were actuated from both cockpits. The instructor could not control the propeller blade pitch. The R-7 prop governors were actuated only from the forward cockpit. The instructor's instrument panel included the airspeed indicator, turn indicator, altimeter, vertical speed indicator, heading indicator and two tachometers. The artificial horizon, oil and cylinder head temperature gauges were installed only in the forward cockpit.

The modification of the aircraft 1-102 (full number: 2201102 – t22 was he number of the factory) was deemed by NII VVS much more successful than the previous slight modification of Pe-2 s/n 5-2 (220502). From autumn of 1942 on short batches of 2 – 5 dual control trainers were produced by Factory No. 22. In this factory they were produced simultaneously with Pe-2R reconnaissance aircraft, which received the first number of the batch. The trainers had the numbers 10 or 20 (ending the batch or the first half of the batch). As the trainer version was built within the production batches, they were fitted with M-105RA engines and other elements typical for combat aircraft. In September 1943 NII VVS completed evaluation of the trainer aircraft s/n 10-231, powered by M-105PF engines, driving WISh-61P propellers. The aircraft, previously referred to as

[120]: Open instructor and gunner/wireless operator cockpits in a UPe-2. The fragment of the digit "1" visible near the checkerboard has similar shape as in two photographs of aircraft number "10". Probably the photo depicts the same aircraft.

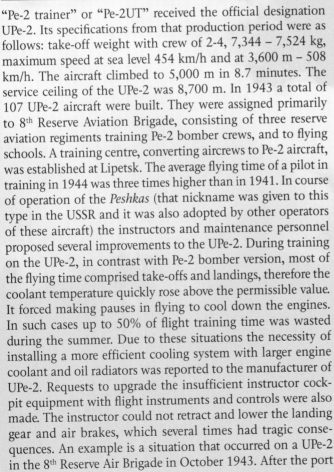

[121-122]: A part of a UPe-2 aircraft, visible in the background, in three-colour camouflage on upper and side surfaces, with the number "4". The section of the fuselage with the number is enlarged. Dęblin 1947.

"Pe-2 trainer" or "Pe-2UT" received the official designation UPe-2. Its specifications from that production period were as follows: take-off weight with crew of 2-4, 7,344 – 7,524 kg, maximum speed at sea level 454 km/h and at 3,600 m – 508 km/h. The aircraft climbed to 5,000 m in 8.7 minutes. The service ceiling of the UPe-2 was 8,700 m. In 1943 a total of 107 UPe-2 aircraft were built. They were assigned primarily to 8th Reserve Aviation Brigade, consisting of three reserve aviation regiments training Pe-2 bomber crews, and to flying schools. A training centre, converting aircrews to Pe-2 aircraft, was established at Lipetsk. The average flying time of a pilot in training in 1944 was three times higher than in 1941. In course of operation of the *Peshkas* (that nickname was given to this type in the USSR and it was also adopted by other operators of these aircraft) the instructors and maintenance personnel proposed several improvements to the UPe-2. During training on the UPe-2, in contrast with Pe-2 bomber version, most of the flying time comprised take-offs and landings, therefore the coolant temperature quickly rose above the permissible value. It forced making pauses in flying to cool down the engines. In such cases up to 50% of flight training time was wasted during the summer. Due to these situations the necessity of installing a more efficient cooling system with larger engine coolant and oil radiators was reported to the manufacturer of UPe-2. Requests to upgrade the insufficient instructor cockpit equipment with flight instruments and controls were also made. The instructor could not retract and lower the landing gear and air brakes, which several times had tragic consequences. An example is a situation that occurred on a UPe-2 in the 8th Reserve Air Brigade in October 1943. After the port

engine failure the crew had to make an emergency landing. On approach to landing the trainee erroneously deployed the air brakes instead of the wing flaps, which ended in a crash because the instructor could not correct this error. Lack of a complete set of flight instruments, including the artificial horizon, in the instructor cockpit hampered flying at night and in clouds. An inconvenient shortcoming for the instructor, particularly in winter, was the necessity to climb on the port wing and walk upwards on a slippery wing to enter the cockpit. The remarks from the instructors arriving at the design bureau of Factory No. 22 and expectations to implement them were deemed right, but also… too difficult to be fulfilled. The designers limited themselves to introducing minor improvements, such as steps to climb on the wing, but significant changes to the Pe-2 were not introduced. Air Force specialists pointed out the necessity to introduce further changes. These included reduction of the airplane's weight by removal of redundant fuel tank protection, forward ShKAS machine gun with ammunition box and armour plates protecting the crew positions, useless in a trainer aircraft, was recommended. Improvement of visibility from instructor's cockpit by shifting it forward and replacement of the solid fairing made of plywood behind the forward cockpit by one of similar shape, but made of transparent Plexiglas. The need to fit the instructor's cockpit with a complete set of flight instruments was emphasized. The possibility of disengaging flight control in the forward cockpit from the instructor's cockpit, to neutralize trainee's errors in flight, was deemed necessary. The need to enlarge fuel tanks to increase the endurance was also considered. However, the factory design bureau and its industrial supervisors were not eager to implement these rec-

Pe-2 and UPe-2 aircraft in Poland

Production Batch Number	Aircraft Number in the Production Batch
Pe-2	
308	10
330	16, 18
331	16
334	17
348	7
350	1, 8
351	3, 13
352	14
353	1,14
354	1, 9, 12, 14, 15, 16, 20
355	4, 10, 13, 17
356	2, 3, 4, 5, 13, 15, 18, 19
357	1, 7, 8, 13, 14
358	7, 14
359	13
361	11
363	4, 15
364	6

Production Batch Number	Aircraft Number in the Production Batch
365	2, 6
366	15
368	4, 5, 7, 8, 14
369	3, 11
370	7, 8, 18
371	1, 8
383	3, 16
387	18
389	2, 5, 6, 7
391	19
392	1, 20
393	11, 16, 17
394	8, 11
395	1, 4, 5, 10, 11, 20
396	1, 6, 13, 17,18
397	1, 9, 17
398	13
399	1, 16, 17, 19
400	3, 4, 9, 18

Production Batch Number	Aircraft Number in the Production Batch
401	6, 8
402	16
403	3
417	6
428	4
433	18
441	4
442	7
493	17
UPe-2	
348	4
354	20
392	20
404	20
418	10, 20
470	10, 15
474	15, 20

ommendations and expectations. The UPe-2 aircraft produced in 1945, from the 179th batch to airplane s/n 10-231, differed only in having VK-105PF engines, individual exhausts, redesigned outlets of coolant and oil cooling air tunnels, antenna mast moved from the back to the front of the trainee's cockpit. Only a few UPe-2 airplanes were fitted with transparent fairings behind the trainee's and instructor's cockpits, increased area of nose glazing and the gunner/wireless operator's position without redundant armour. Armour plates protecting the pilot's and navigator's seat, fuel tank protection and fuel tank neutral gas filling system remained, although these items were redundant in a trainer aircraft.

In June 1945 Factory No. 22 ceased production of the Pe-2 bomber versions. From s/n 5-492 onwards it produced only UPe-2 aircraft. In August 1945 a post-war production UPe-2 s/n 20-501 was evaluated in NII VVS. Since VVS recommendations had not been implemented in this aircraft, it failed to pass the control tests in NII VVS. Its performance did not differ much with those of s/n 10-231, evaluated in September 1943. Production of the UPe-2 ceased in December 1945. These aircraft were operated for a long time along with the UTB-2. In the USSR 93 aircraft were lost in failures and accidents and 17 were scrapped due to wear.

During the training course of twelve Polish dive bomber pilots in the Military Flying School in Engels, USSR, from November 1944 to April 1945, due to shortage of production UPe-2 aircraft a modified Pe-2 bomber was used. One of pilots trained in this aircraft was Kazimierz Wierzbicki, the author of the description of this aircraft. "*The cockpit of this aircraft differed only slightly from the bomber version. Navigator's position – a seat with recess for the parachute – was occupied by the instructor. He was seated in very uncomfortable position, but I never heard him complain. Dual controls were of tiny size and the control column, tilting from the starboard side, with a small steering wheel. Another doubled mechanism, accessible for the instructor, was the rudder trimming wheel. All other flight and engine controls were in the hands of the trainee. One panel with*

a full set of instruments enabled observation of their indications. In genuine dual control trainers the instructor's cockpit was located in the rear, in place of the fuel tank. This untypical conversion of a bomber into a dual control trainer had many advantages. First of all, the airplane's all-up weight was not changed. Moreover, the amount of fuel was not reduced, which allowed more sorties between refuelling. Very important was the fact that the instructor, seated just behind the trainee, could carefully monitor his actions and behaviour. It enabled him to react to trainee's errors much quicker and more efficiently. A serious disadvantage was the aforementioned instructor's seat, particularly unpleasant for him on take-offs and landings".

Colours and markings of Polish UPe-2 aircraft

Two paint schemes could be seen on Polish UPe-2 aircraft. In the 7. PLB the upper wing and fuselage surfaces and the fuselage sides were painted olive green. Surfaces visible from below were painted light blue. The checkerboards were of similar size and situated in the same places as on the Pe-2s. On the fuselage, aft of the checkerboard or on some aircraft ahead of the checkerboard, white one-digit numbers were preceded by the letter S, usually separated from the letter with a dash. Some of the UPe-2 aircraft operated by the Officer Flying School in Dęblin wore the wartime Soviet camouflage pattern. Upper surfaces of the wings, fuselage, engine nacelles, horizontal empennage and vertical empennage, fuselage sides were painted in dark green, tan and dark gray splotches. Surfaces visible from below were light blue. In 1946 the Pe-2 and UPe-2 aircraft operated in Dęblin, after having the red stars on fuselages, tail surfaces and wings painted over, had the checkerboards on forward fuselages, applied during the war in the 1st Bomber Aviation Division, left. In Officer Flying School in Dęblin the tactical numbers were painted in red on the fuselages. The digits of these numbers had various, often decorative, styles and had thin white outlines. During overhauls the Pe-2s from Dęblin were repainted olive green on upper and side surfaces. The lower surfaces were still painted light blue.

[123]: *An UPe-2 with red and white spinners and no dive brakes. A three-ship formation of UTB-2 aircraft is making a low pass over Dęblin airfield. The tail number is erased (a censorship practice of the time). Remains of the number is visible left of the checkerboard. This photograph was faked by the removal of the instructor's cockpit, overflying UTB-2 aircraft and other items, and side nose glazing and other non-existing details were crudely added. The photograph doctored this way was published in 1975 (Ministry of Defence Publishing Office), describing the "special duty version of Pe-2FT multi-role aircraft" developed in Poland.*

[124]: *A taxiing UPe-2.*

[125]: *A group of cadets of the Officer Flying School in Dęblin posing next to a Pe-2. Note bright, probably gray, colour of the aircraft.*

[126]: *Technical inspection of a UPe-2 in the Officer Flying School. The number 10-418, identical to the serial number of one of UPe-2 aircraft, is visible on the ladder.*

[127]: *A UPe-2 of the 1st Squadron, 7. PLB undergoing engine maintenance. The mechanic in the side cap is Adam Wierzykowski.*

[128]: *A UPe-2 from the 7. PLB after a forced landing.*

[129]: Open inspection hatch of the tailwheel retraction mechanism. The checkerboard was painted with a stencil, without filling in the missing fragments.

[130]: A UPe-2 with empty mount of removed VK-105PF engine.

[131]: White spinner of a UPe-2 of the 30. PL MW. The working mechanic is Petty Officer Wójtowicz.

[132]: A UPe-2 with cockpits covered with tarpaulins. The port engine is removed. The mechanic carries the oil tank of the removed engine. Note the non-regulation combination of the mechanic's clothing: jacket with sailor's collar, necktie and Petty Officer rank insignia, quilted trousers and civilian flying cap. Such caps were a popular winter headwear for adults, youngsters and children in Poland in the 1950s.

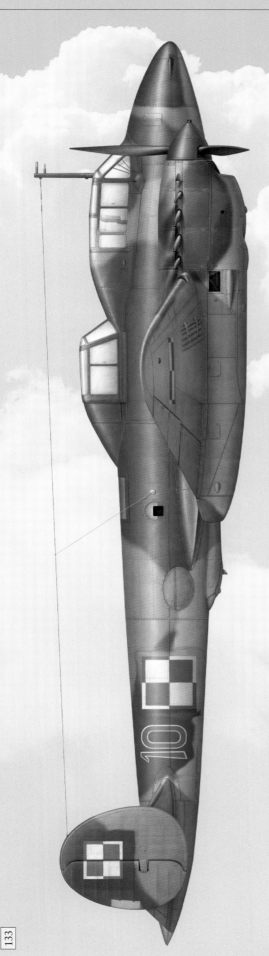

[133]: Petlyakov UPe-2 red "10" of the 3rd Composite Training Squadron of Officer Flying School in Dęblin in 1946. The wartime paint scheme. Characteristic of the early years of squadron's operation are the decorative shape of the red digits with white outlines and red spinners or only their tips, as on this aircraft. The rudder trim tab is yellow. Number 10 its red with white outline.

[134-135]: UPe-2 "10" of the 3rd Composite Training Squadron of Officer Flying School in Dęblin with decorative red digits of the number with white outlines on the fuselage. Second half of 1946.

[136]: UPe-2 white "S3", serial number 4-348 of the reconnaissance-bomber flight of the Naval Air Squadron, based at Wicko Morskie in 1948. Upper surfaces are olive green and the lower surfaces are light blue. The aircraft was transferred from the 7. PBN, thus it initially had red lower sections of the tail fin and spinner tip. The number is white without a dash between the letter and the stylized digit.

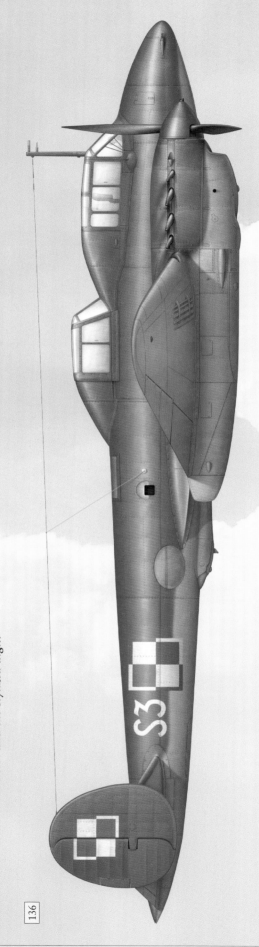

136

[137]: UPe-2 "S3", s/n 4-348 of the reconnaissance-bomber flight of the Naval Air Squadron. The flight's officers and other ranks pose for the photo. The aircraft was previously operated by the 7. PBN, therefore it wears markings typical for this regiment – red lower sections of the tail fins and spinner tips.

137

[138]: Lt Hilary Zanucki in open instructor's cockpit of a UPe-2 from the 30. PL MW. Babie Doły 1952.

138

[139]: Petlyakov UPe-2 white "S-1" of the 7. SPLBN, Ławica 1947. Upper surfaces are olive green and the lower surfaces are light blue. Typical for this regiment red lower sections of the tail fins and spinner tips. The tail number is situated between the checkerboard and the empennage.

[140-141]: UPe-2 "S-1" of the 7. SPLBN damaged when the port landing gear strut collapsed on landing. Lower sections of the tail fins, rudder trim tabs and spinner tips are red. Ławica, summer of 1947.

[142]: Petlyakov UPe-2 white "S-5", Ławica 1950. Upper surfaces are olive green and the lower surfaces are light blue. Tail number placed in front of the checkerboard, The unit markings on the spinners are only red tips. The markings on the tail fins are as in the previous years.

[143]: UPe-2 "S-5" and other aircraft of the 7. PLB undergoing maintenance on the flightline.

Tupolev USB

The USB was developed as a variant of the SB bomber, intended for bomber pilot training. The origins of the SB date back to late 1933, when work on a high-speed bomber aircraft was commenced under supervision of A.N. Tupolev. A.A. Arkhangelsky was appointed the chief designer. The new bomber was designated ANT-40 (from the initials of Andrei Nikolayevich Tupolev). The aircraft soon received a new designation SB (*Skorostnyi Bombardirovshchik*, high-speed bomber), with the number and type of engines added. Initially the designation SB-2M-100 was used. Later the engine designation was often omitted, only the first part of the designation was used: SB-2 or even shorter SB. In Russian writing both these designations appear with reference to the same aircraft. The designers' main task was to build an aircraft attaining as high speed as possible in level flight. In the design process of the SB experience gained during the development and testing of ANT-21 (MI-3) and ANT-29 (DIP) twin engine aircraft of similar layout was used. To reduce drag, a new symmetrical TsAGI-40 airfoil with a 16% thickness-to-chord ratio was employed. All crew compartments were enclosed. The new bomber was a mid-wing aircraft of all-metal construction with the landing gear retracting into the engine nacelles. The corrugated skin of earlier Tupolev aircraft was abandoned. According to tactical and technical requirements issued by VVS, the aircraft was to attain a speed of 330 km/h at an altitude of 4,000 m with 500 kg bomb load. The first ANT-40 prototype, powered by two 730 hp Wright Cyclone F3 radial engines, made its maiden flight on 7 October 1934. However, the aircraft had numerous shortcomings, such as insufficient longitudinal stability and controllability. Soon, on 30 December of the same year, the second ANT-40 prototype with wingspan increased by 1.3 m and

improved flight control systems, powered by 780-hp Hispano Suiza 12Ybrs V-12 liquid-cooled engines, made its maiden flight. During the initial factory trials the speed of 430 km/h at 4,000 m was attained – 100 km/h higher than specified in the requirements. During the first stage of state trials a failure took place. In high-speed flight at low altitude increasing wing vibrations, caused by twisting/bending flutter occurred. This dangerous phenomenon was encountered in the USSR for the first time. Experienced pilot K. P. Kinder recovered the aircraft from this dangerous situation, switching off the engines and making a short climb before landing. The design faults of the ailerons with insufficient mass balance were eliminated and the engines were shifted 10 cm forward. New detachable external wing sections with increased leading edge sweep were introduced and the vertical stabilizer area was increased. Thanks to these modifications the aircraft was exceptionally stable and easy to control throughout the entire flight envelope. It could fly stick-free at any speed. It attained a speed of 418 km/h at 5,300 m. This extensively modified second prototype ANT-40 was sent to Factory No. 22 in Moscow as the production pattern of the SB high-speed bomber. Factory No. 22 had previously manufactured TB-3 heavy bombers with corrugated skin, therefore launching of SB production encountered difficulties. Mastering the use of new materials, such as thin "superduralumin" sheet metal and high-resistance steel alloys, such as chromansil and chrome nickel steel and flush riveting, posed difficulties. Simultaneously production of Hispano-Suiza 12Ybrs engine, in the USSR designated M-100, was being launched under supervision of Vladimir Klimov. The first production SB aircraft was built in No. 22 factory in the first quarter of 1936. It was powered by two 750 hp M-100 engines, driving VFSh

[144]: *A USB Type 2 displayed in an exhibition on the new Mokotów airfield on 7 September 1947. Tying-down lines and tarpaulin slipped off the trainee's cockpit are visible.*

145

[145]: A commemorative photograph in front of an USB Type 2. Coolant radiator air inlets, larger than on a Pe-2, are visible.

[146]: VISh-61B propeller of USB Type 2 aircraft with the spinner removed. Oil cooler air intakes are visible in the leading edge.

146

metal two-blade fixed-pitch propellers. After the completion of factory trials the first high-speed bomber regiments and brigades were equipped with SB-2M-100 aircraft. Production SB-2M-100 aircraft had a larger wing area and heavier take-off weight in comparison with the prototype, carried 600 kg bomb load and the speed was reduced to 393 km/h. In course of the production run the aircraft was modernized and fitted with new M-100A engines, uprated to 850 hp with WiSh-2 three-blade, variable pitch propellers (with two pitch settings – coarse for take-off and fine for cruise). Changes in the gunner/wireless operator's compartment were made. The streamlined canopy, flush with the fuselage and sliding aft in case of enemy attack, was replaced by the MV-3 ball turret (with similar opening system as in the improved MV-5 turret, used in the Su-2 aircraft). The gunner, who previously had to lean out into the airstream when firing, was now protected against the air blast. The ShKAS machine gun was always ready to open fire. An aerodynamic compensator reduced the air pressure on the machine gun barrel and facilitating rotation of the turret. Modernization of the M-100A engine led to the development of the new, more powerful M-103 engine (960 hp). The SB-2M-103 bomber with these engines (known also

as SB-2bis) could carry a heavier bomb load, up to 1,500 kg in the overloaded condition. In the second half of 1939, from the 201st production batch on, the front radiators were replaced by tunnel radiators, which forced the redesign of the engine cowlings. Various SB versions were produced during 1936-1940. Production totalled 6,656 aircraft.

The operation of mass-produced SB bomber aircraft forced the development of a dual control trainer variant. The trainer version of SB-2 was built by conversion of one of the production aircraft from Factory No. 22. An open cockpit with additional flight controls for the instructor replaced the glazed navigator's compartment in the nose. The trainee occupied the unaltered pilot's cockpit. This aircraft successfully completed state trials during 11–16 March. After the completion of the trials a batch of 29 airplanes, designated USB, was produced in Factory No. 22. The instructor's cockpit could also be installed in place of the navigator's compartment in operational units.

As the SB aircraft were withdrawn from bomber regiments, they were converted to USB trainers. The number of SB aircraft converted to trainers out of the production plant is estimated at 81 aircraft.

The first Poles trained on USB aircraft came from the draft ordered by the USSR in pre-war Polish territories, liberated from German occupation from 1944 onwards. They were sent to the military flying school in Engels, where Pe-2 dive bomber pilots were trained. After the completion of the training course on R-5 biplanes, they would accumulate about 15 – 18 hours of flying time on USB aircraft, converted from SB-2M-100A bombers. They practised flying over a rectangular route, in manoeuvering and in formation. Having flown 80 – 100 sorties they converted to UPe-2 combat trainers. In May 1946 the Polish air force received six USB aircraft. Three were referred to as Type 1 and the other three as Type 2. Soon one USB Type 2 was struck off for spare parts. The two remaining USB Type 2 aircraft were sent for overhaul at No. 2 Aircraft Repair Facility in Bydgoszcz.

USB Type 1 aircraft had engine nacelles of cross-section shape fitting to the large oval of the front radiators of the M-105RA engines, as in the SB-2M-100A aircraft. Large front area made an impression that the aircraft was powered by radial, not V engines. The larger upper part was the coolant radiator and the smaller lower part the oil cooler. The propeller shaft ran through the middle of the coolant radiator. A thermostat controlled operation of the radiator louvres. The sliding canopy of

the gunner's compartment was initially glazed. Later this glazing was painted over or replaced by sheet metal, as can be seen in the photos. The aircraft had single-strut, shock-absorbing landing gear, with the wheel mounted on a single fork. They were very war-weary, with most of their service life expired, and there was a shortage of spare parts. One airplane was made in 1937 and two in 1939. These aircraft had unserviceable landing gear retraction mechanisms, thus the landing gear was locked in the lowered position and additionally braced with struts, as used in the version with skis. Lack of spare parts for these aircraft, production of which ended in 1940, made keeping several aircraft systems serviceable impossible. Automatic pitch control mechanisms of the VISh-61B propellers often failed, therefore the propeller pitch was permanently locked in an optimum setting. Only in 1947 were the weary engines of all five USB aircraft replaced by new VK-105RA engines.

USB Type 2 aircraft, despite being powered also by M-105RA engines, differed from Type 1 aircraft in having streamlined engine nacelles. The cowlings with tunnel radiators had aerodynamically refined shape, with reduced cross section area. The engine nacelles with large, bottom air intake had fixed, non-adjustable section of the radiator air inlet duct. Cooling was adjusted by a movable lower air scoop, adjustable in flight. The oil cooler was installed in a tunnel inside the wing and the air was supplied via inlets on the leading edge of the inner parts of the detachable wing sections. The USB Type 2 aircraft had the MV-3 turrets on the gunner's position, with the guns and aerodynamic compensators removed, which is visible in preserved photographs. The glazing of the unused turrets eventually lost transparency and became dim.

Five USB aircraft of both types, assigned to the Officer Flying School in Dęblin in May 1946, remained in its inventory for a brief time, but during 1946 – 1948 airworthy airplanes were temporarily used for crew training in the 7. SPLBN at Ławica airfield. In Dęblin they were used for taxiing and straight take-off training. They were rarely used for short flights between airfields. USB aircraft of both types were displayed on 7 September 1946 at the new Mokotów airfield in Warsaw during a military and civil aircraft exhibition. One USB Type 2 was severely damaged during an emergency landing at Dęblin airfield in the summer of 1946. Two USB aircraft were destroyed by a hurricane, which swept over Dęblin airfield. According to Capt. Kazimierz Gawron's account, in the summer of 1948 engines of a USB Type 1 were started and the commander of the 2nd Squadron in the Dęblin school, Maj. Koptyev, made one flight in this aircraft, observed by the cadet pilots. They remembered that the engines of this aircraft were very noisy and their sound did not resemble that of Pe-2 engines, which was familiar to them. One USB stood in the hangar of the Officer Flying School in Dęblin among a couple of Pe-2 aircraft, used for cadet pilot training. The then cadet Paweł Gawron describing it paid attention to its engine nacelles, in which *"the radiators looked like in an old automobile"*. This suitable description shows well the character of these radiators, often referred to as "honeycomb", as fitted to the USB Type 1.

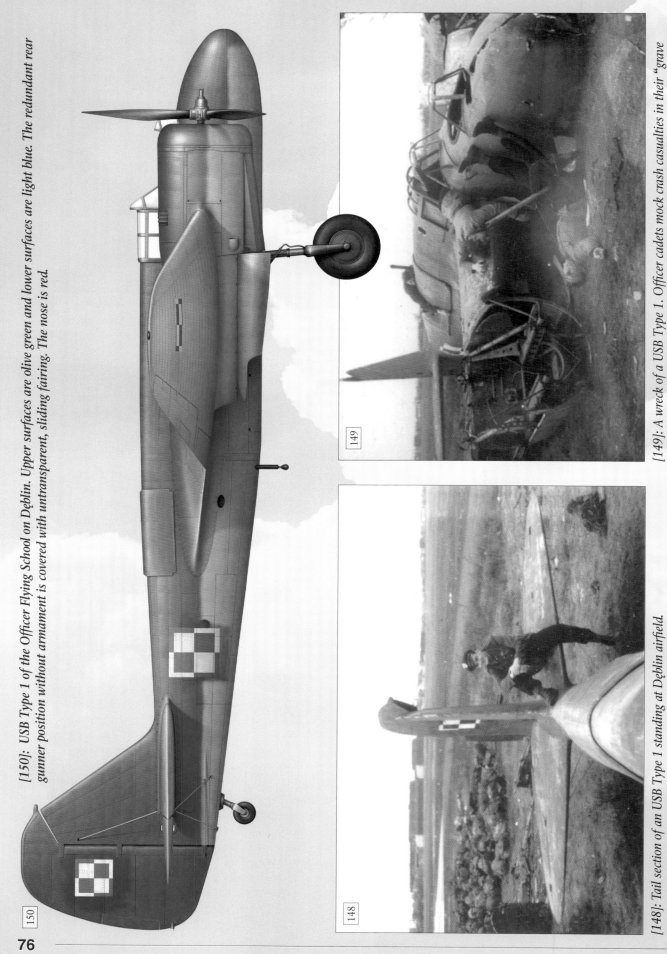

[150]: *USB Type 1 of the Officer Flying School on Dęblin. Upper surfaces are olive green and lower surfaces are light blue. The redundant rear gunner position without armament is covered with untransparent, sliding fairing. The nose is red.*

[149]: *A wreck of a USB Type 1. Officer cadets mock crash casualties in their "grave joke". Probably this is one of two USB aircraft destroyed by a hurricane at Dęblin airfield.*

[148]: *Tail section of an USB Type 1 standing at Dęblin airfield.*

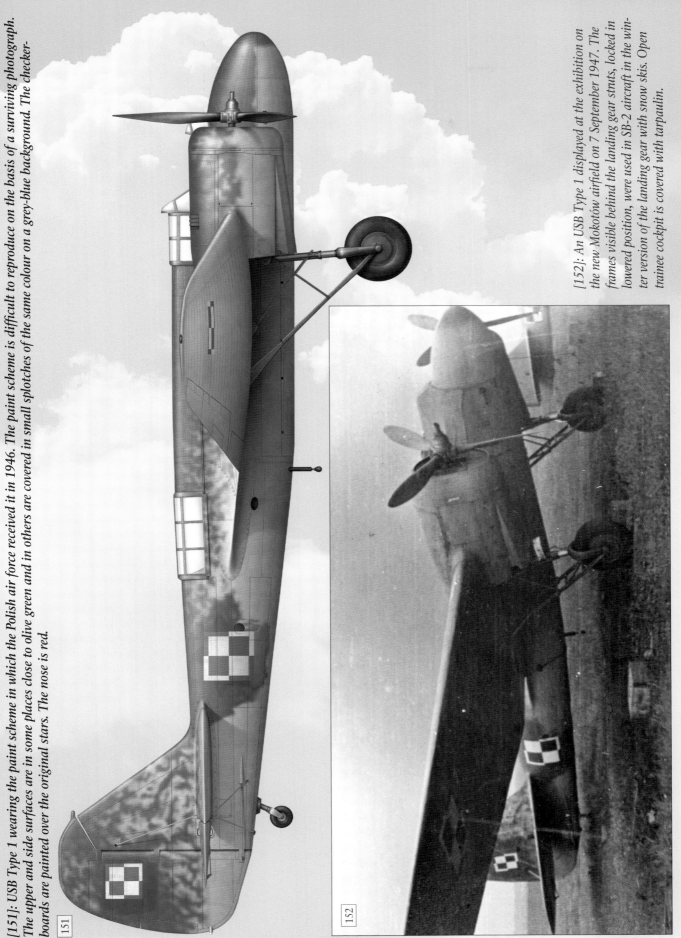

[151]: USB Type 1 wearing the paint scheme in which the Polish air force received it in 1946. The paint scheme is difficult to reproduce on the basis of a surviving photograph. The upper and side surfaces are in some places close to olive green and in others are covered in small splotches of the same colour on a grey-blue background. The checkerboards are painted over the original stars. The nose is red.

[152]: An USB Type 1 displayed at the exhibition on the new Mokotów airfield on 7 September 1947. The frames visible behind the landing gear struts, locked in lowered position, were used in SB-2 aircraft in the winter version of the landing gear with snow skis. Open trainee cockpit is covered with tarpaulin.

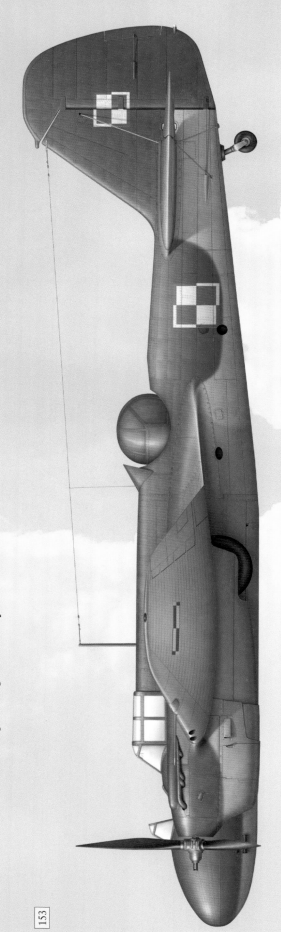

[153]: *USB Type 2 of the Officer Flying School. Upper surfaces are olive green and lower surfaces are light blue. The checkerboard is placed untypically, half on the rudder and half on the vertical stabilizer. The inoperative gun turret is painted over.*

153

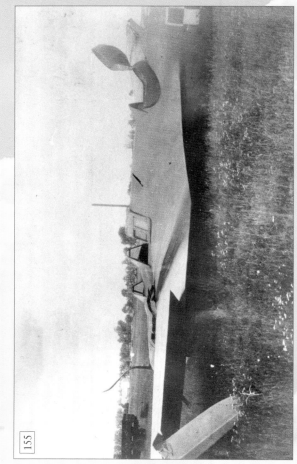

155

154

[154-155]: *A USB Type 2 after a forced landing. Raised hatch of MV-3 gun turret is visible. Dęblin, summer of 1947.*

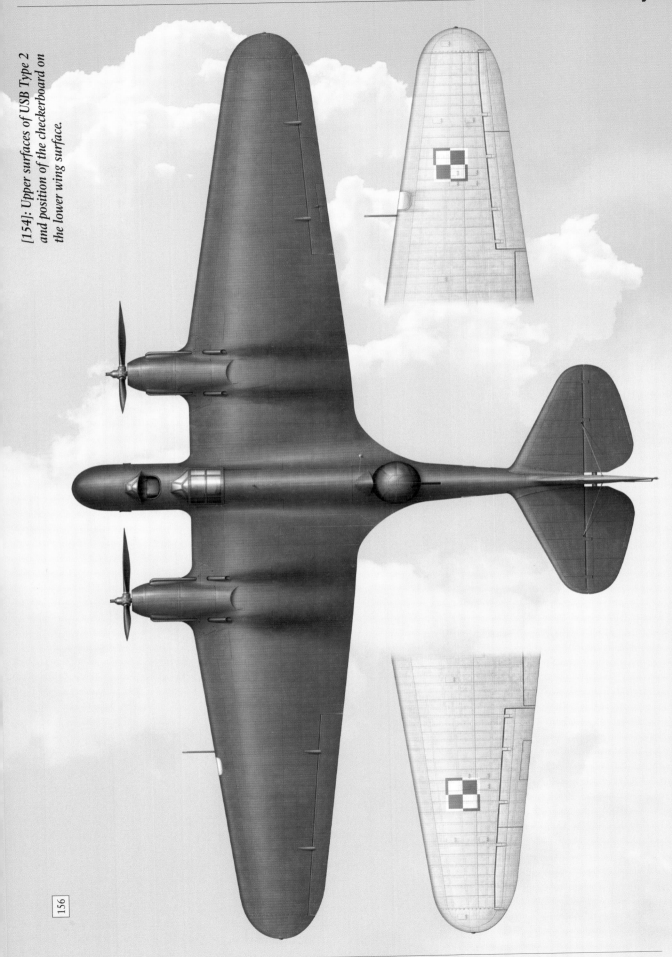

[154]: Upper surfaces of USB Type 2 and position of the checkerboard on the lower wing surface.

156

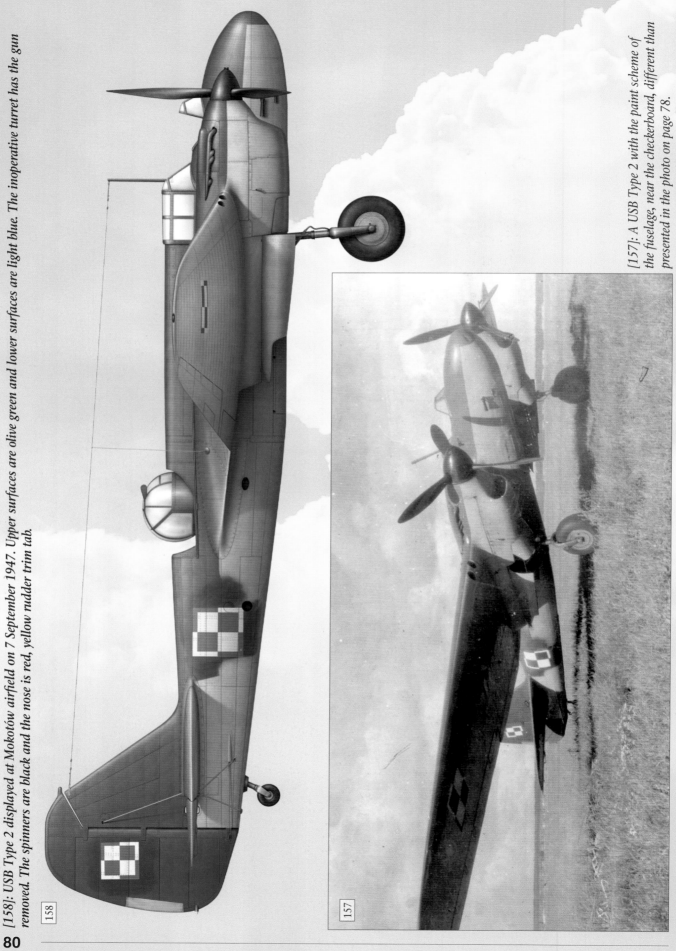

[158]: *USB Type 2 displayed at Mokotów airfield on 7 September 1947. Upper surfaces are olive green and lower surfaces are light blue. The inoperative turret has the gun removed. The spinners are black and the nose is red, yellow rudder trim tab.*

[157]: *A USB Type 2 with the paint scheme of the fuselage, near the checkerboard, different than presented in the photo on page 78.*

158

157